How I Survived Single Parenting
and
Lived to Tell About It!

Benita Louise

A GrateFul Hands Creation

Published by
GrateFul Hands, LLC
Tulsa, Oklahoma

Book Cover Concept: Benita Louise

LCCN 2009927310

ISBN-10: 0-615-29570-3
ISBN-13: 978-0-615-29570-1

Printed and bound in the United States of America

Dedication

To my son, Raymond,
your unconditional love and understanding
of the true meaning of family, has helped me to become
a wiser mom and a stronger woman of faith.

Contents

Acknowledgements

To my son, Raymond, your wonderful sense of humor and unwavering faith helped me to laugh during life's many challenges.

To my parents, Rev. Elbert Hyche, Jr. and Odell Neal, thank you for the sacrifices you made and the love you gave to all your children. Most importantly, thank you for teaching us about the love of God.

Thank you to my nephew, Jeffrey V. Sanders, (who I have nicknamed "The Wiz") for sharing your brilliant talents to edit and critique this book. I truly appreciate you for graciously opening your home and sacrificing your time to bring this manuscript to publication. I couldn't have completed this book without you.

To Demechra Davis (Meechie), thank you for allowing me to turn many Sunday dinners into conversations about this book. You listened patiently, gave me guidance, and never once complained.

To Carla Farmer, (I don't know where to begin), thank you for allowing me to vividly share my dreams and for always knowing the exact words to say. Your ideas, direction, and assistance in writing this book helped me to stay focused on its true purpose. I truly appreciate your wisdom and prayers in helping my vision unfold. Your friendship was definitely appointed by God, for such a time as this.

Thank you to all my family and friends for always believing in me. Your encouragement, support, and inspiration kept me going. You were definitely the wind beneath my wings.

To Darryl Washington and Kenneth Sanders, Jr. (Ken-J), your guidance and encouragement of my *Parenting Newsletters* gave me the courage to pursue the completion of this book. The dedication of your time, support, and ideas in writing this book were crucial. Words cannot express how much I appreciate both of you. Darryl, thank you for keeping me on my toes! I owe you big time!

I extend my sincere thanks to authors Hannibal B. Johnson, Devetta Arnold, and Rose Hammond. Thank you for sharing your wisdom and knowledge on self-publishing. Because of your unselfish giving, lives will be changed. Rose, because you generously gave your all, you helped me cross the finish line, and I am truly grateful.

To Carla Farmer, Carolyn Sanders, Demechra Davis, Jenny Hardridge-Finley, Paula Sharp-Diggs, Rhonda Kaye Brock, Rozena Currin, and Wanda Finley-Thomas, thank you for stepping in at the twenty-fifth hour to use your talents and gifts to proofread this manuscript. I was genuinely touched by the way you treated this book as though it was your own. Because of each of you, this process was a blast!

Beloved, I pray that you may prosper in all things and be in health, just as your soul prospers (3 John 1:2).

Author's Forethoughts

I NEVER THOUGHT at forty-eight years of age I would be at "this place" in life. If only someone would have told me life would be like *this*!

Occasionally, these thoughts would occur after dealing with a challenging situation that aroused my emotions. From childhood to adulthood, the struggles along life's journey created fears and distorted beliefs that deeply penetrated my soul.

Whenever single parenting became overwhelming, and the pain of life became too unbearable, I would become frightened, and my emotions would inevitably take me on a rollercoaster ride. During these times, I often found myself running back to the image of June Cleaver, on the television sitcom *Leave it to Beaver*, who represented peace and tranquility to my wounded soul.

Over the course of time, the unrealistic perceptions I developed from what seemed to be "effortless parenting" between June and Ward Cleaver, led me to believe that life should be a bed of roses. Because I expected the conditions of life to always be perfect, parenting for me was an enormous challenge!

Destiny

I find myself, running from myself, trying to find myself
Longing to break free from me.
As I struggle to escape this shell,
I find it's just as hard staying in, as it is trying to get out.

I can see what's up ahead,
But the clouds of despair often block my view.
No one seems to hear the screaming
Coming from deep within my soul.
I dare not tell anyone,
For no one could comprehend the depth of my pain.

I've been here before. The pain is the same.
The darkness lingers like midnight, for a thousand years.

Was this day written in God's plan?
The birthing of His promise is at hand.
Everywhere I turn, His purpose surrounds me,
Covered in obscurity
With the code written only in my being to unlock my destiny.

Slowly, my destiny unfolds, as when the sun peeks through the clouds,
and in a brief moment is hidden again.

I find myself, running back to myself,
Hoping to find solace there, from the darkness behind the clouds,
Only to find the sun beckoning me to escape, and come out for another
Glimpse of the destiny that awaits me.

◡◡◡

Introduction

WHEN I INFORMED Aunt Almeda I was expecting, she expressed with sheer excitement, "I sure hope you have a boy!" Not knowing what she meant by this, I traveled through many months of morning sickness, divorce, a second marriage, and then, a single mom again with my son by my side. It took over twenty years to understand the actual meaning of her words. Apparently, Aunt Almeda knew that through the different phases life would bring, a boy would make me strong.

During my son's young adult years, the effects of my own personal issues, along with my lack of parenting skills, reflected in his rebellious behavior. The pain that was hidden deep within his soul from not growing up with his father's guidance and direction, resulted in him making unwise and imprudent choices.

I started this book at least five times over the years; and each time, I wanted to write some great introduction that would lead my readers to believe that I was perfect at being a single parent and raising a perfect child. But after experiencing six months of tumultuous challenges because of my son's behavior, and finally coming to the realization that parenting is about training a child to become a healthy, responsible adult, I can now share, *"How I Survived Single Parenting and Lived to Tell About It!"*

෴

My desire is to bring awareness to parents of the various causes for their children's negative behavior. This book is not designed to be a step-by-step guide to parenting, but provides real life examples that illustrate how a child's negative behavior can be closely linked to the parent's lack of parenting skills, as well as unresolved issues within the parent and the child.

The "Life Lessons" in this book are life changing, and will inspire parents to equip their children to become healthy, responsible adults. Whether parenting a nine year old or guiding a nineteen year old along their journey, these lessons are designed to help minimize stagnation in development, and maximize growth and independence.

To My Son,
Age 3 ½

You're always into something.
It seems you just can't keep still.
The way you run and jump around is very much unreal.

You used to be so cuddly.
You would sleep the whole day long.
I'd sit and watch you fall asleep, while singing you a song.

When I held you in my arms,
I would talk and you would coo.
I would make funny faces, and you made some too.

Now, when you fall asleep, it takes more than a song.
Now, you do more than coo, you can talk the whole day long.

That cuddly baby I often miss is now a cuddly boy.
Despite all your mischief,
You will always be my joy!

Chapter 1

✦

THE SPACE SHUTTLE
Scattered Pieces

MY FRIEND, PAULA, and I had no business talking about birth control pills; especially since neither one of us knew how they really worked in the first place. And besides, my doctor never *clearly* stated that the effects of the pill only last for twenty-four hours. I only remember her casually saying, "Just make sure you take the pill the same time everyday."

During our excited conversation about birth control, Paula had enthusiastically stated, "After you've been on the pill for a while, it takes at least six months for it to get out of your system!" Little Raymond definitely proved *that* theory wrong! Eight months later, he pushed his way into this world and has been pushing every since!

✦✦✦

Although I hadn't planned on getting pregnant so soon after marriage, Little Raymond was my pride and joy. My husband and I separated one month before he was born, so naively, I went to the lawyer's office to file for a divorce.

"Honey, you're pregnant!" the lawyer abruptly stated. "This is not a good time for you to file for a divorce!"

"Is your husband beating you?"

"No!" I answered bluntly.

"Is he running around on you?"

"No, I don't think so!"

"Well, what's he doing with his paycheck?"

Now crying, I tearfully answered, "He usually takes twenty dollars and gives me the rest!"

"Well baby, as long as he is paying the bills you don't have anything to worry about. You go on home, and if you still want a divorce after you have that baby, come back to my office and we'll talk about it."

"I'm seven months pregnant!" I thought to myself. "What does he *mean* I don't have anything to worry about?"

After I collected myself, I held my head high and quickly walked out of the lawyer's office. I knew there was no way I'd ever go back to him for *any* kind of advice, especially after his array of perfunctory questioning. Sadly, I was forced to accept the fact that it was not a good time to file for a divorce.

A few weeks later, my husband decided to move back to California. Because I was devastated, I began to mentally prepare myself to give birth without him by my side. But the emotional stress of being separated, prematurely pushed me into labor, and propelled me on a journey that would lead me to fulfill my destiny and purpose.

❦❦❦

After our son was born, Raymond's father decided he wanted to stay in California. He also wanted us to get back together and work things out. But by this time, Derrick, a long time friend, had been spending time with me and comforting me during this traumatic season in my life.

One night, out of nowhere, Derrick kissed me on the cheek. "What did you do that for?" I asked in amazement.

"Because I wanted to," Derrick responded nonchalantly.

Now, I was really confused. I knew Raymond needed his father, but Derrick was making advances, that secretly I really wanted and enjoyed.

Without discussing my feelings with Derrick, I decided to move to California. I didn't tell him my plans until the night before I left. Although I knew my marriage was really over, the desire for my son to be raised by his father overshadowed my true affections. I never told Derrick that my love for him had blossomed in my heart.

♪♫♪♫

Once my son and I arrived in California, I unpacked our things and found a place for them in our new home. I didn't realize the marital problems we had in Oklahoma had traveled to California, also. I wildly imagined they were hidden in the baggage that was stored underneath the plane, and these problems comfortably found a place in our home as well.

After three months, when things didn't work out, I left California and moved to Oklahoma City. I stayed with my friend, Denise, and her parents, and was too ashamed to tell my family I had left Raymond's father.

A month later, when my sister Carol found out I was back in Oklahoma looking for a job, she hightailed it to Oklahoma City and picked us up.

"Girl, you don't need to be staying with those people! They are *not* your family!" she stated dramatically, as though I had hitch-hiked my way back to Oklahoma and had been taken in by strangers.

Carol lived in a small town that was definitely not on my "most favorite cities to live in" list, so when I couldn't find a job I wasn't too upset. Once again, I packed up my son and moved to Tulsa to stay with my friend, Michelle. Derrick and I magically picked up where we left off, and started spending time together again.

By the time Raymond was five months old, the money I had saved began to run out. Still not having a job, I became afraid and secretly applied for food stamps. "This is *definitely* not the life I had planned. I'm a college graduate on food stamps. How can this be?" I asked myself.

To make matters worse, one day I unknowingly lost some of the food stamps, and Michelle found them.

"Benita, I found some food stamps outside. Are these yours?" Michelle asked.

Being too ashamed and too proud to admit that I needed help, a flat out, "No!" was my quick reply.

My son and I needed food and shelter, and I had too much pride to live off the "system." Afraid I would be found out, three months later, I reluctantly moved back to California. Again, leaving Derrick behind, it felt as though my heart was being ripped right out of my chest. I knew this time I would lose him forever. I hid the pain of living without him, deep within the labyrinth of my soul.

·ℐ·ℐ·ℐ

Raymond's father was a great provider, but that wasn't enough to make me happy. Although I felt he didn't know how to be a husband, one thing I knew for sure was that he loved his son. Wherever he went, little Raymond was close behind. Whenever I saw them together, this picture became enough to satisfy me, and soothed my pain from the sacrifice I had made in leaving Derrick behind, again.

As time passed, I began to learn the ways of a Californian. Raymond's father and I took many trips to Oakland and San Francisco to make sure I would be comfortable driving across the Bay Bridge. My first job interview was in San Francisco on the fourteenth floor of a building that overlooked the Bay. The magnificent view of the water was to die for. "Now this is what I call living!" I said to myself.

Eventually, I found a job as an accounts payable clerk at a lumber company that was only a few blocks from our home. Raymond's father worked nights, so I spent a lot of time with my friends, Carmen and Marva, who I had previously met in college. We often frequented exclusive restaurants that were along the San Francisco Bay. The tranquil waters always seemed to sooth my wounded soul.

To pass the time, I often went to the Bay alone and watched the para-sailors ride the wind before splashing down into the peaceful waters. With a broken heart, I would sing along with Otis Redding on the radio. I was indeed wasting time, wasting my life, and missing Derrick.

෴෴෴

I didn't know how long I could keep up the charade of being happily married. Almost daily, I begged God to give me a sign if I should stay in California or move back to Oklahoma. Like Alice, in *Alice's Adventures in Wonderland*, asking the Cheshire Cat which way she should go, I desperately needed direction for my life.

Raymond's father continued to provide for us, but he also continued to go out partying and leaving me at home alone. One night while he was at the club, I packed my bags and hid them in the closet; as if God was going to give me instructions to grab my son and flee in the middle of the night.

After several weeks passed, God still hadn't given me a sign. He was taking His sweet time, so I decided to take things into my own hands. I bought a plane ticket and made plans to leave in seven days.

For the whole week, I continued with my normal routine. On the last day, while Raymond's father was at work, I lugged all my bags down the stairs of our two-story townhouse and threw them in the car. I had previously made plans to spend the night with my friend, Liz, who was going to take me to the airport the next morning. But for some reason, I decided to go to the carnival in Oakland before I went over to her house. (*Raymond was not quite two years old and asleep in the stroller, so what could I have possibly been thinking?*)

After I walked around for awhile, I finally mustered up the courage to call Raymond's dad from a payphone to tell him my plans.

"I'm leaving you," I said reluctantly. "I'm going back to Oklahoma and my plane leaves tomorrow."

"Stop joking!" he responded with confidence, as though he knew for sure I wasn't going anywhere. "No, you're not!"

"I know, I'm just kidding," I said hesitantly. "April fools!"

As I reached out to hang up the phone, I looked up into the sky at the people on the roller coaster ride. I could see their arms swinging in the air and the excitement on their faces, but the only voice I could hear was the one in my head.

"April fools! Is that the best you could do? Now who's the fool? He will be off work soon, and you will have to beat him home, put up all your things, and act as though nothing happened."

I slammed down the phone, and drove home as though I was trying to win the *Indianapolis 500*. Once I arrived home, I took everything back into the house and hid the bags in the back of the closet. When Raymond's dad came home, he had no clue I had been on a wild rollercoaster ride that had nothing to do with the carnival in Oakland.

After two weeks, my bags were still hidden in the closet, and I was still waiting for a sign from God. One evening I noticed Raymond's dad had ironed his partying clothes before he went to work. I guess he wanted to make sure when he came home he could quickly change and leave for the club without missing a beat.

When he came home from work, I asked him to stay home so we could talk and spend some time together. I told myself, if he said no, this would be the sign for me to leave and go back to Oklahoma.

Raymond's father expressed he had no intention of staying home that night, and my cry for attention failed to penetrate his heart. Two weeks later, I left California and promised myself I would never, ever return.

✎✎✎

Raymond's father eventually moved back to Oklahoma. It had never crossed my mind that Raymond's dad could still be a father to him without the two of us getting back together, so I made one last attempt to make our marriage work.

Although we got back together, we never resolved our issues, and after several agonizing months, I was desperately ready for our rollercoaster marriage to be over. I had finally realized that I had to first save myself, before I could be the mother my son needed me to be.

Raymond's father moved out right before Christmas. He offered to stay until I got a job.

"No thanks!" I said, with a whole lot of attitude. "We'll be *just* fine!"

A few months later, when he decided to move back to California, my heart broke. "He could at least stay in Oklahoma to help raise his son," I thought to myself. "Over the years I tried to make sure Raymond's father was in his life, now *this!*"

Raymond's father hadn't planned to file for a divorce before he left, so I knew in order to regain my freedom I would have to move quickly to close this chapter of my life. I didn't have much time to look for a lawyer, but while looking through the television guide, I saw an advertisement for inexpensive divorces.

On my way to the lawyer's office, the radio announcer stated that the Space Shuttle *Challenger* had just exploded.

I convinced myself that this sad moment in history was a sign for me. As the lives for the astronauts had ended, life for me with Raymond's father had also ended. Our "college love" was not strong enough to protect our marriage from the forces that came against us. Like Humpty Dumpty, all the king's horses and all the king's men couldn't put our marriage back together. We were once inseparable, but now our love was in scattered pieces.

Raymond was almost four years old when his father and I divorced. We were too young and immature to be married in the first place. We had no idea how to be husband and wife, or even parents, for that matter.

With little thought of the effect our divorce would have on our son, I pushed Raymond's father away when he tried to kiss me goodbye the day he left for California. Raymond stood close by my side, showing no emotion, unaware that he wouldn't see his father again for over two years.

Because I considered God the head of our home, to me, my family was still complete. That day, I adamantly determined I would be the best single parent ever!

I prayed,

"Dear Lord, I will teach my son about You. Please teach him how to be a man."

Life Lesson #1

Flight attendants consistently remind parents, "In case of the loss of cabin pressure, please put your oxygen mask on first before you assist your children." Likewise, in order to receive optimal results in raising children to become healthy, responsible adults, parents should make it a priority to seek healing and wholeness for themselves.

Single Parenting

I AM DETERMINED
To conquer this thing
Statistics call
Single Parenting!

This challenge is real,
And that's a fact.
Not a play, nor a game, not a one scene act.

I've got the front seat to this real life drama.
My child is the main character.
I'm the daddy and the momma.

Raising my child alone won't be easy,
But I don't have time to feel sorry for me.
His life, not mine
Is in jeopardy.

This is one challenge, where I won't accept defeat.
This is one statistic, whose odds I'm going to beat.
He's my flesh, my blood, and I hope time will tell,
From a babe, I raised him well!

Chapter 2

⚬

DEFINING MOMENTS
Establishing Independence

IT SEEMED AS though the journey of single parenting was suddenly thrust upon me when Raymond's father moved over a thousand miles away. Like a mother bear attacking her prey to feed her baby cubs, I was driven by determination and a strong faith in God to conquer the challenge set before me.

Raymond was a very energetic child and always wanted a lot of attention. He didn't like to play by himself; therefore, I spent a lot of time entertaining him. I hadn't equated his rambunctious behavior and his desire to always have me close by, with him missing his father. Because he was so young when his father left, I automatically thought if I was strong, my son would be strong, too.

When Raymond turned six, I planned a trip for him to go visit his father for the summer. I wrote my phone number in all of his books, and made sure he knew how to dial my number if he wanted to come home.

Raymond's father and I agreed to meet in Bakersfield, California. Bakersfield was almost twenty hours away, so I persuaded my sister, Carol, and her husband, Kenny, to go with me and help me drive. Because I knew I couldn't drive across town and pick Raymond up once he was with his father, these were the longest hours of my life.

As we got closer to Bakersfield, I silently prayed that Raymond would not want to leave me. After all, I was the one that sacrificed for him these past two years! I prepared his meals and nurtured him back to health when he was sick! "How could he possibly want to leave *me*?" I asked myself.

But in spite of my rationalization, when Raymond saw his father, he was the happiest kid in the world. He clung to him like a pair of socks with static cling that just came out of the dryer.

After we ate breakfast, Raymond kissed me goodbye. He acted as though this was a normal weekend visit that had been taking place for the last two years. Even though my greatest joy was for Raymond to be with his father, I began to fear his father would not know how to take care of him. Would he make sure Raymond ate breakfast each morning, played games with him, and read to him before he went sleep each night? Would he tend to our son like I did?

Over the next three weeks I could hardly sleep. With Raymond being so far away, his absence made me feel as if there was a hole in my heart and a part of me was missing. I didn't know if I could handle the whole summer without seeing him. I was hurting, but I knew he had been hurting for two years, and needed his father more than I needed him to be with me to satisfy my fears.

After a month, Raymond called and said he wanted to come home. His father had disciplined him for the first time since he had been there, and he was afraid. Although I had done my best not to interfere, I was missing my son. His cry to come home was just what I wanted to hear.

I quickly planned a trip to pick Raymond up. Within the next few days, I was on the road again. Deep within, I wondered if I was really rescuing Raymond, or saving myself from my own fears.

✎✎✎

Raymond's elementary school years were really a challenge. Because of my desire for him to succeed, each night I would spend several grueling hours helping him with his homework. Little did I know he was becoming dependent on my help.

Each year Raymond would wait until the last minute to start his science fair project. As usual, I would jump right in and do most of the project for him. After becoming annoyed with his procrastination one year, I asked him why he waited so late to start his project. "Mom, I knew you would help me," was his candid reply.

On the evenings Raymond didn't have any homework, he would read to improve his skills. To make sure he understood what he read, sometimes I had him to read the same story twice. Occasionally, I would set the clock to see how long it would take him to finish. One night when he completed his reading with noticeable improvement, I asked him how he finished so quickly, and he enthusiastically stated, "Mom, I didn't stop at the periods!"

ﾉﾟﾉﾟﾉﾟﾉﾟ

In search of better schools, I enrolled Raymond in Lincoln Elementary, a school that was not in our district. Although I used my friend, Linda's address, I struggled with this untruth. I asked God to forgive me, but continued to act as though we lived in the neighborhood.

My friends, Jackie and David, also lived in Lincoln's school district. Some mornings, I took Raymond's bike over to their house, so he could ride to school with their son, Dakarai.

Because I wanted Raymond to experience life like other boys with a father in the home, I made many decisions based on my own fears and desperation, which unknowingly created other issues.

Life Lesson #2

As the caterpillar must push to overcome the cocoon experience, its passion for growth and freedom causes it to miraculously emerge as a beautiful butterfly. Nature has designed its appropriate time for transformation—a moment too soon would impede the butterfly's growth, and it would inevitably die.

Excessively helping my son with his homework, picking him up early from visiting his father, and changing his schools were all defining moments in his life. Although I thought my actions were helping him, I was actually hindering his growth; therefore, he developed an unhealthy dependency on me.

When children are taught to deal with difficult situations, they develop independence and confidence. When they learn from the challenges that life brings, the valuable lessons can help guide them successfully through life.

Poem, From My Son
Age 8

all I want to say is
thanks you
for all you
done for me
here is a little
Poam
Roses are red
Violtes are blue
I am happy becouse
I am blessed with you

Chapter 3

꧁

MOTHER'S DAY
Underlying Issues

THERE WEREN'T MANY boys on our street Raymond's age, so he didn't get a chance to participate in the usual neighborhood games children play. Because I had this "*Leave it to Beaver*, June Cleaver" perception of life, I always wanted him to be clean as a whistle. His real fun and excitement came when he stayed with my sisters, who lived an hour away.

When Raymond stayed with my sister, Carol, for the Fourth of July one summer, she called me in a panic because Raymond had blown up some frogs with his firecrackers. Evidently, she had become attached to the frogs that made their summer home in her yard each year.

On another occasion, when my father took Raymond with him to visit my sisters, I received a startling phone call that Raymond had been shot. My father failed to mention it was a BB gun, so frantically, I called my friends and they were at my house in no time. A few minutes later, my father called back and said the doctor popped the pellet out, and that Raymond was doing fine.

No one could ever explain exactly how Raymond got shot. I was originally told that my nephews, Ken-J and Anthony, had been outside shooting at birds, and that Ken-J thought Raymond was a bird. Each year the story changes and the real truth of why Ken-J shot Raymond is still a mystery.

Raymond always enjoyed staying with my other sister, Brenda, and her husband, Leroy. Even though Brenda had eleven children, I could only imagine that her husband's authority in their family was a key factor in the reason she always seemed to stay calm despite any challenging situations in their home. Once while he was visiting, he was playing with his cousins and tore his scrotum while climbing a fence. He kept it quiet all day, but later in the evening one of his cousins finally told my sister what happened. You guessed it, another startling phone call.

My friend, Rhonda, and I went to pick Raymond up, but not before stopping to buy some spicy chicken wings before we left. (*I know you're wondering why I stopped to get something to eat before tending to my son. By now, I was used to the fire drill, and I knew if he was with either of my sisters, he was in good hands*).

After we arrived, we took Raymond straight to the emergency room. Because I couldn't stand the sight of needles or my son in pain, I stayed behind the curtains while Carol bravely held his hand as the doctor stitched him up.

ᴥᴥᴥ

During third grade, Raymond gave his teacher a constant challenge. Because he was always energetic and often disturbed the class, I frequently met with her to discuss solutions to help him keep focused.

Raymond's school counselor recommended that he attend a summer camp program that was designed to help children learn to interact with others. Although going to camp was a great opportunity for him, I felt his disruptive behavior in class was his way of crying out for his father. The only antidote for his behavior was his father's love.

While Raymond was at camp, he participated in activities with other boys his age and experienced camping outside and exploring nature. When I picked him up, his cabin leader gave me the following note: "Raymond was very energetic. He is a true leader. Hopefully, he will learn how to pick up after himself before he returns next year." Because this camp turned out to be a wonderful experience, Raymond attended for the next five years.

✒✒✒

Although Raymond's father was not a consistent part of his life, I never talked negative about him. Raymond was already having a hard time coping with not being able to see him on a regular basis, and the last thing he needed was for me to bad-mouth his father. I knew criticizing his father would only make it harder for them to build a relationship.

I knew Raymond's father really loved him, but I also knew he had challenges of his own. Sometimes he would send Raymond's birthday gift late, so to make Raymond think his father sent his gift on time, I would buy a card, put some money in it, and give it to him the day of his birthday.

In many single parent homes, birthday gifts and child support payments are few and far between from the absent parent. Although Raymond's father helped out financially when he could, most of the time, it was just enough to get by.

When he moved back to California, I had candidly expressed to him, "If you are going to be a part of your son's life, you need to be a great father, especially since you live so far away!"

Maybe this statement was too harsh and impractical, but I wanted him to be like Ward Cleaver. Ward always provided love, care, and discipline for Wally and the Beaver, but Raymond's father could not live up to my expectations. How could he? He had his own personal issues to deal with. But even though I knew this, it still didn't change my expectations of his role as my son's father.

One year, Raymond's father sent him some money for Christmas to buy a Nintendo set. I bought the set for him, but a week later I had to take it back to the store because I needed the money for food. I discussed this with Raymond, and despite him wanting to keep the game, he seemed to understand.

Because I had too much pride to show that I was in need, it was hard for me to ask for help. Although times were tough and money was scarce, I never thought we were poor. To me, poor was only a state of mind. I strongly believed: *when one is down to their barest necessities, their true riches are found.* Although there was never a time we were without heat and electricity, during the hard times I learned to trust in God to provide for us.

⁓⁓⁓⁓

Whenever I visited Carol, I would often search through her cabinets and refrigerator for food, as though her house was the neighborhood grocery store. Because her refrigerator was always overflowing, I was like a kid in a candy store. "One day, I'm going to have plenty of food, too," I would tell myself, while getting a package or two of meat out the refrigerator to take home.

Carol always laughed when she saw me leave with a bag of food. She never acted as though it was a big deal, and I never let her know my true desperation. "Girl, I haven't been to the grocery store yet," I would say jokingly. I was too proud to let her know that I was having hard times.

To save money, whenever Raymond and I went out to eat, we shared a meal or both ordered a kid's meal. After he got older and began to eat more, he no longer wanted to eat only a half portion. But of course, that didn't stop me from trying to convince him to share a meal. Somehow he always found a way to gently remind me, "Mom, I'm bigger now."

Because my focus was always on saving money and surviving, rather than actually eating and getting full, I quickly found a new way to save money. I began to buy regular portions and only eat half the meal, saving the other half for the next day. (*After doing this for many years, this habit was woven into my psyche, and the real damaging effects were ingrained in my soul*).

I always believed my mother's survival skills and my father's work ethics were established in me at an early age. A sense of great pride was also rich within our family's blood, and this pushed me to survive. Because I was so determined to conquer single parenting, I unconsciously internalized my own pain and was hardened to my emotions.

⁓⁓⁓⁓

Although Raymond and I never talked about it, I knew he desperately missed his father. I didn't understand the depth of the pain he felt when he was almost four years old, and saw me push his father away the day he left for California. Nor could I fathom the pain and emptiness he would possibly experience the rest of his life, by not having his father to help him develop into the man he would one day become.

The day Raymond's father left, his bright eyes and bubbly expression turned into a solemn gaze. With each passing day, I could plainly see that not being able to see his father afflicted him severely. Even though I loved my son dearly, my love for him could not take the place of his father's love.

Raymond internalized his pain because his father was not a consistent presence in his life. Because he didn't have the capacity to analyze and effectively communicate his pain, his cry for help came through his disruptive actions at school. Spankings only temporarily stopped his unruly behavior, because his behavior was coming from the pain deep within his soul.

ᔍᔍᔍ

As I watched the news, I began to notice that whenever there was a traumatic incident at a school, the school would rush counselors in to talk to the students. The commentator explained that the counseling would minimize the negative effects of the trauma on the students' lives.

Raymond had actually been traumatized the day his father left. Until the news discussed the effects that traumas have on our lives, I didn't know Raymond needed counseling to help him deal with the pain of missing his father. How could I? After all, I had unknowingly internalized my own pain and didn't know that I, myself, needed counseling. As a result of Raymond's pain, his negative behavior began to escalate, and I began to feel that I couldn't handle the responsibility of raising him alone.

One weekend when I took Raymond to stay with Carol for a few days, before I dropped him off, I asked her if she and her husband would raise him. Although I loved my son, I felt if he had two parents, it would minimize his pain. Because the picture of June and Ward Cleaver so effortlessly raising their sons together was ingrained in my mind, I was willing to give up my son, so he would have the benefits of being raised with a mother and father in the home.

Ironically, it was also Mother's Day weekend. When I went to church that Sunday, the Pastor explained that children are blessings from God, and that God designed each parent specifically for their children.

"Even though the struggles of parenting may seem never-ending," the Pastor enthusiastically stated, "every sacrifice a parent makes for their child, is priceless!"

I was so excited about the message that I jumped up, left church early, and drove straight to my sister's house to pick up my son. This time, stopping to get those delicious spicy chicken wings was not my priority. I had realized God purposefully created *me* to be Raymond's mother. Even though I knew there would be many challenges, I was determined and committed to be the best mother ever!

Life Lesson #3

Whenever children experience trauma, their internal afflictions are often expressed through their external actions. Effectively discussing these traumatic experiences with a counselor can bring healing and resolve for underlying issues.

Chapter 4

✍

PLAYING HOUSE
Unacceptable Behavior

RAYMOND ATTENDED PRIVATE school from fourth through eighth grade. Because of my desire for him to acquire a good education and have a solid Christian foundation, I sacrificed buying certain luxuries to provide this for him. I strongly believed a Christian school would help enforce the spiritual teaching I implemented in our home.

Raymond and I usually had Bible study once a week. During this time, we read the Bible, prayed, and also sang praise and worship songs. Because I wanted to impart a strong faith in my son, I often acted out dramatic illustrations of the Christians in the Bible. I took the chance of him thinking I was a little crazy, to show him how to apply the Word of God to his life. One time when we were both tired, I asked him if he still wanted to have Bible study, and he earnestly replied, "Although I'm tired mom, we should have it anyway, because most likely, I really need it."

I felt I was strong in my faith, but evidently my oldest brother, LeGrande, didn't think so. He lived in California and often sent me Christian pamphlets and tapes. Apparently, he didn't believe I had the "mountain moving" kind of faith to overcome life's challenges.

Sometimes he would call me sporadically to see if I had read my Bible.

"LeGrande, I don't have time to read the Bible today," would often be my smart-alecky response.

"Well, what are you doing now?" he would ask, like he was my daddy or something.

"I'm on the phone talking to a friend."

"If you would stop talking on the phone so much, you would have plenty of time to study your Bible!"

Sometimes he would call and catch me off guard by asking me to pray. I would always give him an excuse why I couldn't pray, because I was too embarrassed.

"One of these days you are going to *have* to pray on the spot, and then, what are you going to do?" He asked authoritatively.

I didn't really understand his comment and didn't give it much thought, until two o'clock one morning when Raymond began to shake uncontrollably and complain of stomach pains. It was really cold and dark outside, and I was afraid to leave the house to take him to the hospital. At that moment my brother's words came to mind, and I immediately began to passionately pray. A few minutes later, Raymond stopped shaking and went back to sleep. I knew right then, the next time my brother called and asked me to pray, I would gladly comply without hesitation.

⋰⋱⋰⋱

As Raymond grew older, I wanted him to be able to talk to me about anything, so I established weekly meetings to discuss issues and plans for the week. Even though this was a great idea (*at least I thought it was in the beginning*), he began to debate with me and always wanted to prove his point.

Because I didn't have a balance when discussing issues with him, he thought it was okay to express himself no matter the situation. When discussing this with my friend, Daniel, he emphatically expressed to me, that I was "playing house."

"You're the parent and he is the child. He doesn't have to know why you do *anything!*"

◦◦◦◦

Raymond's fourth grade year was off to a good start with a new Christian school, new atmosphere, and yes, a different teacher. When I first met Raymond's fourth grade teacher, she sparkled with enthusiasm to the point of tears. She was just out of college and stated with sincere affection how much she loved the students. "Oh, no!" I thought. "My son is going to change her mind *real* quick!" But during the school year, somehow Raymond won her over, and the fourth grade ended with much success.

Raymond played soccer, tee-ball, and basketball during the summers. He also attended summer day camp programs at the community centers. The summers were a time I cherished because Raymond's personality seemed to be a lot more relaxed. The daily study routines were something we were both happy to do without.

During fifth grade, Raymond became pretty comfortable with his teachers. He made friends easily, but his study habits and organization skills were below average. Although he was able to read, his reading comprehension was not on his grade level. Because he didn't always understand what he read, he would lose focus in class.

Raymond started getting in trouble for talking and leaving his seat without permission. His playful behavior took the attention away from the fact that he didn't understand his work. Because he stayed after school frequently for detention, the teachers and the counselors saw me quite often.

◦◦◦◦

Although Raymond had challenges in school, the school still allowed him to go on the mission trip to Mexico. His teacher felt this would be a life changing opportunity for him.

While he was in Mexico, he ministered to underprivileged children and was able to see children living in extreme poverty. After he came home, he asked if he could take a few canned goods to school to give to the poor. I gave him permission to do this for one day, but by the end of the week our cabinets were empty. He had continued to take food each day without my knowledge. When I asked him why he took all of our food to school, he said he wanted to help feed the poor.

Raymond's trip to Mexico was an eye opening experience for him. I noticed after he returned home, he had developed a giving heart. But despite his giving heart, it was evident in his attitude that his father not being around still troubled him severely.

☙❧

The school year grew more challenging as Raymond continued to get in trouble for speaking his mind. When his class went on a field trip the last week of school, his teacher told him to stop talking. Raymond told her he didn't have to because she couldn't tell him what to do. Because of his actions, he was suspended the last three days of the school year.

Before school was out, I met with Mr. Joseph, the assistant principal, about Raymond's suspension. He had seen me on several occasions meeting with Raymond's teachers because of his behavior. Mr. Joseph told Raymond that he had exceeded the number of detentions and should be put out of school, but because he admired my attitude and personality, he would allow him to come to school in the fall.

✒✒✒

At the beginning of the Raymond's sixth grade year, I was not employed. I had been terminated from my job and began receiving unemployment benefits. I also worked a part-time job to help make ends meet. I was able to pay Raymond's tuition for the first semester of school, but by the middle of the next semester, I was behind in paying his fees. I wasn't sure how I was going to make the payments, but I knew that somehow God would provide a way for me to pay his tuition.

During the school year, several of Raymond's friends had stopped going to the school. Their parents had gotten a divorce and could no longer afford for them to attend private school. Raymond became concerned that he was going to have to change schools, too. Knowing that God had always supplied our needs, I emphatically expressed to him, "God *will* provide for us!"

I went to Mr. Joseph to discuss the situation. (*Yes, the same Mr. Joseph that showed favor to Raymond when he was suspended the last three days of school*). I explained to him that I had lost my job and would pay the tuition once I received my tax refund. Mr. Joseph prayed that I would receive my tax refund expediently, and also for God to bless me with the job I desired.

Mr. Joseph prayed for me on a Friday, and three days later I received my tax refund check. I also began a new job shortly after, and paid the rest of Raymond's tuition in full.

Life Lesson #4

Often, parents overlook unacceptable behavior in their children and label it as a "cute and innocent" display of character. This display of character will develop (please let me repeat), *will develop* into more serious character flaws and eventually create challenges for the parent and the child.

Behavioral patterns are established at an early age. If negative behavior is not effectively addressed, children will think their behavior is acceptable and will carry their negative behavior patterns into adulthood.

Chapter 5

✑

LIFE SKILLS
Life Skills

PARENTS DO NOT intentionally set out to damage their children's self esteem or cause them to be crippled in their development. But sadly, unbeknownst to parents, children are adversely affected by the parent's unresolved issues and lack of parenting skills, and often become stagnate in their growth.

Negative behavior consistently repeated in children usually implies that previous issues were not resolved effectively. Sometimes parents are not equipped with the adequate skills to correct the problem. The sad truth is that parents do not realize negative behavior is inevitable in their children when unwise parenting practices are used.

There may be many books written on parenting, but there is not a one hundred percent "fool proof book" which can guarantee that a child will be successful and fulfill the purpose for which he/she was created. Because writers know the full responsibility of the parent and child's welfare belongs to the parent, books on parenting do not have a warranty stating:

If you do not see changes in you or your child within thirty days by using the methods and techniques described in this book, you may return this book to your nearest store for a full refund.

Writers can only bring awareness to parents, and at the same time hope that the parents sacrifice the time needed to acquire effective parenting skills.

∽∽∽

As I tried to shelter Raymond from the harmful elements of the world, I explained to him that listening to secular music was not good for him. But of course, he didn't agree.

"A lot of my Christian friends *and* their parents listen to this kind of music!" he stated convincingly.

My response was definitely biblical, but not necessarily balanced. I dramatically expressed to him, "In the Bible, if God would have found one righteous person, He would not have destroyed the two cities Sodom and Gomorrah!"

Raymond looked at me with a puzzled look on his face, but I continued. "If God was looking for one family that didn't listen to secular music, wouldn't you want to be the family to save our whole city?"

Of course Raymond didn't fall for any of that at all. So, the next Sunday after church was over, I pushed through the crowd to talk to my Pastor, like the woman in the Bible with the issue of blood, who pushed through the crowd to get to Jesus for her healing. I knew that secular music could have a negative effect on the mind of an innocent child, so I was determined to do everything in my power to remove the influence of this music from my son's hearing.

"Pastor," I said in hysterics, "my son wants to listen to secular music! Please tell him this music is not good for him!"

I'm sure somewhere in the back of my Pastor's mind he thought I was a little over the edge. Thank God he overlooked the display of my desperate emotions and wisely responded. Instead of telling him it was wrong to listen to secular music, he prayed that the effects of listening to the music would not be damaging.

My pastor knew it was unrealistic for Raymond to never listen to secular music. He understood the negative influence came from the words and the meaning of the song, so he cautioned me to pay close attention to his music.

◦◦◦◦

When the atmosphere around our children is filled with many negative influences, our children suffer greatly. The music industry, Hollywood, and our education system all play a big part in the mental health of our children. No private school, no matter how great the education, can shelter them from the real enemy — "The Poisoning of a Child's Mind."

The destructive mental imprints our children face each day are detrimental to their success. If the old saying: "You are what you eat," is true, doesn't the same truth apply to the saying: "You are what you think?"

◦◦◦◦

During the summer, I spent a lot of time thinking about how Mr. Joseph prayed for me to find employment and for my finances to be blessed. The fact that God answered his prayer so quickly really amazed me.

"I should have asked Mr. Joseph to pray for God to send a husband into my life. When I see him again, that's *exactly* what I plan to do," I said, as I chuckled to myself.

The following school year, I often saw Mr. Joseph in the halls, but would be too afraid to ask him to pray that God would send me a husband. I felt he might think it was silly for me to ask such a thing. Usually, when I got the notion to pursue something, my emotions would drive me up the wall until I accomplished what I had originally set out to do.

After several months passed, I finally gained the courage to go to Mr. Joseph's office, and boldly stated my request.

"Mr. Joseph, you prayed for me and God blessed me with a new job. Can you pray that God will send me a husband?" Mr. Joseph did exactly that!

A few months later, I met my future husband, Michael. After eighteen months, Michael and I married. When I first saw Raymond experience a father/son relationship with Michael, I was truly overjoyed. Michael had two younger sons from a previous marriage. Although Raymond was a teenager, he seemed to like the idea that he now had a "real" family. When the four of them interacted, I felt God gave my son the family he had desperately longed for.

Even though I was very independent after being single for over ten years, I was eager to let Michael take the lead in our home. I knew he wanted the best for Raymond, so I also gave him the authority to make decisions in regard to his discipline. Although I didn't always understand his parenting methods, he taught me about "life skills."

Michael thought I was sheltering Raymond by sending him to a private school. He also felt my method of parenting was hindering his growth.

"Raymond is not developing the appropriate life skills he needs," he expressed with much concern. "These skills are developed by learning from life's challenges and will teach him how to survive in the world."

As Michael continued to watch my parenting style, it was obvious to him that my parenting method was not effective. He often became frustrated with me because I permitted Raymond to hang out with his friends even though his grades were below average. This puzzled him and he definitely wanted to know why I allowed this.

"Sometimes I am really exhausted and need a break," I expressed to him, while trying to hold back my tears. "I need some time to myself so I can relax. Deep inside, I feel I am the one being punished when I make him stay at home."

Although Michael understood my dilemma, he strongly suggested that we find a balance that would allow me to get the rest I needed, as well as implement consequences to Raymond for his low school grades.

Michael pointed out, that as a single parent I allowed Raymond to get away with making unwise choices. This lack of discipline caused him to develop a casual attitude about life, which resulted in his day-to-day tasks being completed with mediocrity, doing just enough to "get by."

As I was strongly determined to be a great mother, Michael also demonstrated this same passion in making sure Raymond acquired "life skills." Although our beautiful Cinderella wedding had portrayed the love we had hoped to share for a lifetime, my marriage to Michael lasted less than a year. Despite this difficult time in our lives, I gained valuable insight on "life skills" and became a much wiser parent.

ᔓᔓᔓ

Children are not robots assigned with model numbers, nor do they all learn the same way. Although each child has limitless potential, each child's "environment" will be instrumental in dictating his/her level of success. In this case, "environment" does not mean external factors, but the knowledge and understanding of "life skills," and the ability to implement them effectively.

It is evident a child's external surroundings doesn't always predict whether a child succeeds. How is it that some children raised in low income housing communities successfully become entrepreneurs, doctors, or lawyers? Although these children may have lived in less than desirable conditions, I must conclude—their emotional foundation was strong and their self-esteem was preserved. Without a doubt, their parents made sure they were equipped to conquer life's challenges by teaching them effective "life skills."

Paradoxical as it may seem, children who are raised in wealthy families and live in homes guarded by iron gates are not automatically safeguarded from life's challenges. Without "life skills," every child is susceptible to becoming homeless or living in poverty as adults.

Life Lesson #5

The ability to reason and make wise decisions is developed in childhood. When children are rewarded for positive behavior and reprimanded for negative behavior, they become conscious of their choices. The choices they make are significant because their decisions will become their future reality. As they learn "life skills," they also become aware that every unwise choice has a corresponding consequence.

Chapter 6

❧

THE ANSWER IS IN THE VILLAGE
Developing Healthy Relationships

A S I WALKED past Raymond's room, he was laying in bed with the blankets tightly wrapped around him. At that moment, it seemed as though God was trying to get my attention to alert me of this critical season in his life.

The weather was far too nice for an energetic teenager to be asleep on a Saturday afternoon. But like a bump on a log, Raymond was still in bed instead of outside playing basketball with his friends. And, I *definitely* didn't like the picture I saw.

I began to seriously analyze this perplexing image. I knew Raymond was still in pain; I could sense it. I understood he was still hurting from his father not being in his life, but I couldn't allow this to be an excuse for him to let the pain overtake him and steal precious moments from his life. I knew from that moment, God did not want me to allow my son to live a mediocre life. I felt God had impressed upon my heart, that I demand Raymond walk in excellence.

Without a doubt, Raymond needed his father in his life to give him direction, but I knew this wasn't going to happen anytime soon. I thought to myself, "Perhaps a role model, a male who could be his mentor, could help mold and shape him as he becomes a man."

I began to pray,

"Dear Lord, I thank You for helping my son walk in a spirit of order, discipline and self control. I thank You for causing Your purpose to prevail in his life, and teaching him to walk in excellence. My deepest desire is for him to be a man after Your own heart."

This was a prayer I prayed almost daily. These words helped me get through my son's teenage years. No matter the circumstance, I held on to my belief that God *would* answer my prayer.

∽∽∽

Over the years, there was very little communication from Raymond's father. Raymond needed a role model, but there were too many factors involved. Trying to find someone I could trust, or someone that had the time and desire to be a mentor, was quite a challenge.

As I talked to others, I hoped they would see my desperate cry for help and offer assistance. Not wanting to put anyone on the spot, I didn't think it was appropriate to come right out and ask, "Will you be a role model for my son?"

I had often heard the old adage: "It takes a village to raise a child." As I pondered this statement, the lack of role models for our children definitely began to puzzle me. After much reflection, I realized that the idea of molding a young life can be a frightening thought, and that everyone is not equipped to be a role model. Therefore, with great sadness, I concluded that perhaps something is wrong with the village. Sometimes our personal issues make it hard to provide assistance to others; however, as we individually seek to resolve our issues, we are able to reach out to help others, and then, the village can be healed.

∽∽∽

I was awakened to the harsh reality that Raymond may never have a mentor to help him navigate through manhood. I knew the effects of not having a positive male role model would carry over into every area of his life, and create issues, that he would eventually have to overcome. As I covered up my pain from this reality, Raymond also hid his pain behind his insensitive attitude.

Raymond was at a point in his life that he desperately needed to hear his father say, "I love you son!" The absence of his father had created subterranean scars in his soul that had an adverse affect on almost every decision he made. These scars, at the core of his being, predisposed limitations to his inherent growth. In fact, the sad truth is that in order for Raymond to assertively move forward in his life, he would need to forgive a person he didn't really know, his father.

I was at a place I had never been before in my understanding of Raymond's pain. With this understanding, the task of effective parenting became more critical to me than ever before.

·✌·✌·✌·✌

With a strong determination not to fail, I continued to intensely pursue my challenge as a single parent. My pain was so excruciating, that sometimes I cried within myself. I didn't want Raymond to see me in agony, and I never wanted him to know that I was hurting because I couldn't give him what he needed the most, his father.

Raymond didn't make it any easier for me. He did things most children do to test their parents. He skipped school, stayed out later than curfew, and of course had an attitude with a capital "A."

When I wasn't sure how to handle a situation, sometimes I would frantically call my friend, David, who lived in Oklahoma City. Although he never physically disciplined

Raymond, the advice he gave me through the years was instrumental in how I implemented the consequences to Raymond's for his actions. He was able to give me a man's perspective, and always knew the right words to calm me down and talk me through the problem.

My cousin, Darryl, was very straightforward whenever I called him for advice. He always informed me when my explanation to solving a problem wasn't logical. Again, by listening to a male's perspective, I was challenged to re-think the disciplinary action that I wanted to give to Raymond for his inappropriate behavior.

⚮⚮⚮

After Michael and I divorced, Raymond and I moved into a one bedroom apartment. I gave Raymond the bedroom and I slept in the living room on the daybed. Because he was a teenager, I felt he needed his own space, especially when his friends spent the night. I wanted things to be as close to normal as possible, but actually, how could your mom sleeping in the living room be anywhere close to normal?

Raymond attended the high school that was in our district. He adjusted well, met new friends, and was a model student. I was so excited when he came home and did his homework without asking me for help, that it brought tears to my eyes. When I was married to Michael, Raymond changed schools and attended a private school that had a self-paced curriculum. This method of learning taught him how to study independently, a skill he lacked because of his dependency on me during his elementary years.

Close to the end of the first semester, Raymond's teachers began calling me to discuss his behavior. He was not turning in his homework and was playing around in most of his classes, so I went to the school to meet with all of his teachers for a conference. *(I had become a pro at this)*.

When I arrived, the teachers were already sitting around a large table. As I took my seat, it appeared they were intimidated with my presence, possibly because of previous unpleasant experiences with other parents.

As the teachers each stated their concerns about my son, I realized they were not demanding excellence from him. They had been letting him get away with unacceptable behavior and not turning in his homework all semester. Raymond always knew when to turn on his charming personality, and he was definitely using it to "get over" on his teachers. I will admit I, too, had often been bamboozled by Raymond many times, allowing him to get away with negative behavior instead of disciplining him for his actions.

Evidently, Raymond's charming personality caused his teachers to overlook the fact that the semester was almost over, and only called me when they realized it was part of the school policy, not necessarily because of concern for him. (*They must have known there was no way he would be able to make up the homework he missed, so what was the point of their phone call this late in the game?*)

At the end of our meeting, I kindly, but firmly expressed to his teachers: "Under no circumstances are you to allow him any special privileges. You *must* demand he follow the rules. When he doesn't, please give him consequences for his actions." (*Of course this was a speech I heard over and over again from Michael when we were married. I guess it had finally sunk in*). The teachers willingly agreed to my suggestion, but acted shocked, as though what I stated was a new phenomenon.

∙◊∙◊∙◊∙

Although Raymond played basketball for the school, he rarely invited me to the games for fear I would shout his name from the bleachers. I'm sure he vividly remembered me running up and down the soccer field when he was six and seven years old cheering him on. I guess he thought I would repeat this embarrassing behavior in front of his friends. I didn't complain much because when I came home from work, I was usually exhausted and wanted to stay home and relax.

Close to the end of the season, Raymond decided to invite me to a game, only because he wanted me to talk with the coach. He and the coach weren't getting along, and he thought the coach was not giving him enough playing time. As I watched the game, I made sure I kept my composure. I didn't want to give Raymond any reason to not invite me to any future games.

In my opinion, Raymond played a reasonable amount of time, but of course I didn't know anything about the rules of the game or playing time for the players. I talked to the coach afterwards and expressed Raymond's concerns. (*Now this would have been a great time for a male role model to stop me from questioning a coach about the way he managed his team*). This questioning only hurt Raymond's chances of having more playing time for the rest of the season. I don't know how I could have forgotten that he was no longer six years old playing basketball for the YMCA. At that age, the coach played each player the same amount of minutes no matter if the player had skills or not, and each team won a trophy at the end of the season whether the team won or lost.

Raymond had been working for McDonald's and saved up money to buy his grandmother's 1986 Chevy Nova. He wasn't thrilled about buying her car, but he knew this was his only means of transportation to get to work and to school functions. Unfortunately, I didn't know that Raymond having a car was going to open up the door to a whole new set of challenges.

One of Raymond's friends, Caleb, also lived in our apartment complex. His mother was also a single parent.

One evening when Raymond spent the night with Caleb, around midnight, he came back to our apartment to get some of his things. When he knocked on the door, I got out of bed and unlocked the door. At the time, it never crossed my mind that he didn't use his key. I got back in bed and reminded him to be sure to lock the door when he left.

After thirty minutes passed, I still hadn't fallen asleep. I remembered that I didn't hear Raymond lock the door, so I got out of bed to see if it was locked. Surprisingly, the door was still unlocked. "Why would he knowingly leave me home alone without securing the door?" I grumbled. "What could he be thinking?"

The more I thought about Raymond leaving the door unlocked, the madder I became. So, I decided to call him to get an explanation for his thoughtless actions. (*Geez, it was one o'clock in the morning, couldn't this have waited?*)

I anxiously dialed Caleb's number, but didn't get an answer. When I couldn't reach him after several attempts, I got dressed to go find Raymond and give him a piece of my mind. By this time, I was angry, scared, and determined to let him know how I felt.

Caleb and his mother, Hannah, lived several buildings down from us. Somehow I mustered up the courage to walk down the dark jogging path to their apartment, rather than drive my car. Once I arrived, I softly knocked on the door, but no one answered. I rang the doorbell, but still, no answer. I went to the side of the apartment to Caleb's room, which could be entered through a sliding glass door. As I peeped in, I saw the room was dark and empty, so I quietly entered.

I prayed softly,
   "*Lord, please don't let anyone shoot me, mistaking me for a burglar.*"

Being led by the light coming from another room, I softly tip-toed through the house, but there was still no sign of life anywhere. As a detective hunting for clues to solve a crime, I anxiously searched for Hannah's bedroom.

After a few minutes, I spotted a closed door that I desperately hoped was Hannah's room. At first, I knocked softly on the door, but as I began to panic, each knock grew louder and louder.

When Hannah finally opened the bedroom door, I anxiously explained to her that I couldn't find the boys. Being a strong woman of faith and seeing that I was worried, she immediately began to pray. As she prayed, I felt reassured that God would bring our boys home safely, and I began to feel at peace.

After Hannah finished praying, she noticed a sack in the corner filled with clothes. A video tape without a label was also sticking out of the sack. As she put the video tape in the player, we looked at each other curiously, wondering what could possibly be on the tape.

We watched the tape for a few minutes and fast forwarded past the "World's Strongest Man" portion. When the boys walked in, the "Dancing Girls" segment of the video was playing, and they were extremely shocked.

Caleb immediately began to explain that they were out throwing eggs at each other. When Hannah questioned him about the tape, he said it belonged to his friend, Greg. She asked him if they watched the girls dancing, and he insisted they fast forwarded that part. But of course I didn't believe *that*! I was so thankful God brought our boys home unharmed, that I didn't ask a lot of questions.

When we returned to our apartment, I explained to Raymond the severity of his actions. And, to help him remember to never leave me at home without making sure the door was locked, I clearly defined his consequences.

At any other time, I would have been fired up, and Raymond would have really gotten a piece of mind. But because I was exhausted, I groggily stated, "You can't drive your car, participate in any school activities, or hang out with your friends for thirty days." And then, I used every ounce of energy I had left, to crawl back in bed.

Life Lesson #6

It is imperative that parents are acquainted with their children's friends, and vitally important for parents to interact with each other and establish open lines of communication to discuss issues relating to their children.

As parents, we can't automatically expect role models to come forth and foster our children. For guidance and support, we can pursue healthy relationships with other parents.

Chapter 7

DIFFERENCES
Parenting Styles

GROWING UP, I distinctly remember the masculine sound of authority in my father's voice. Just like E.F. Hutton, when daddy spoke, everybody listened. Daddy didn't have to say anything twice. We all knew by the tone of his voice he meant business.

During my younger years, my two sisters and I slept in the same bed. Because I was usually afraid to fall asleep, I always wanted to sleep in the middle. My sisters would tell me that the middle was the pee hole, so I would scoot close to one sister, but she would push me back to the middle of the bed. Then, I would scoot near the other sister, but would find myself back in the pee hole again. This went on night after night, until daddy walked past our room and heard us. "Y'all better be quiet in there!" he firmly shouted. Walla! Just like magic. No more nonsense. No more noise. We immediately adjusted our actions and went straight to sleep.

One night when daddy came home, the kitchen was a total mess. Although we were sound asleep, he made us get out of bed to clean it up. We whispered comments under our breath, but no one challenged his authority. He distinctly had the male voice of authority often missed in single parent homes.

Daddy definitely believed in spankings. He would spank us, and then, tell us to be quiet. Sometimes he would talk to us as he spanked us, with each word having a corresponding swat, telling us what we did and that we better not do it again.

One day, when my sister, Brenda, came home late from school, daddy became furious. He told me to go outside and get a switch. Hesitantly, I went outside and picked a switch that was light as a feather. He wasn't very satisfied with the one I chose, so he went outside and picked one himself.

◦◦◦

I can't remember momma spanking us very much; she left the discipline up to daddy. As LeGrande tells it, "Whenever we did something wrong, momma would always tell us, 'Just wait until your father gets home!'"

When I was about five years old, I pretended I worked in a store by putting prices on the canned foods with a can opener. The can opener sounded like the pricing guns the clerks used in the grocery store. Obviously, this sound intrigued me, so I paid no attention to the hole I punched in the can. I don't know how long it took momma to find out, but when she did, she held a mock court session to let my sisters and brothers decide if I should be spanked for ruining the food.

Momma sat me in a big red chair that looked as though it was designed for the Jolly Green Giant. She was the judge and my siblings were the jury. She proceeded to tell them what I had done and asked them if I should get a spanking. My two sisters said no, but my two brothers said yes.

Momma sent me upstairs, and told me to think about what I had done. In the meantime, my sisters told me to put books in my pants so the spanking wouldn't hurt. When momma finally came upstairs, she pretended to spank me, and I pretended to cry. I guess she felt sorry for me, because she knew I had no idea of the damage I had done.

That wasn't the case with daddy. He never tolerated any foolishness. One day, my father told my brother, Dale, to take me to school. Dale was taking a long time to get dressed, and when I begged him to hurry up, he paid me no attention, so I became angry.

"I'm not going to school!" I shouted, while I stomped up the stairs to go to my room.

"You better come back down here!" Daddy yelled right back, while standing at the bottom of the staircase.

"I am so mad!" I muffled under my breath, as I stomped back down the stairs.

"You better get in that car and go to school, or I am going to stomp you into the floor with this broom!" daddy shouted.

Out the door I flew! I was mad at my brother, but more afraid of my father. I'm sure my father would have never stomp me into the floor, but this was his way of letting me know that I was *not* in control.

◦◦◦◦

Over the years, I had allowed Raymond the freedom to speak his mind when we communicated. As a result, we spent many years disgruntled, frustrated, and confused. We could barely have a conversation without it turning into a shouting match—me shouting and leaving the room, leaving Raymond in bewilderment wondering, what the heck just happened?

After years of anguish, I became fed up, pissed off, and angry. Not at myself, not at my son, but at the situation. I knew there had to be a change, and because I was the parent, it was my responsibility to make this change happen. I also believed the change had to take place in me first, so I began to analyze myself to see how I contributed to the ongoing discontentment in our home.

I was sure this change was definitely not going to happen

over night. The effects of the hurt and pain from the many arguments we had through the years were not going to suddenly "poof" and be gone like magic. There was no Houdini to put our hurt in a box and cause the pain to suddenly disappear. I definitely knew the harmony I desired between the two of us, was not going to appear out of the blue. It was going to take sacrifice and hard work for this much needed change to take place.

I was convinced that over the years Raymond had become hardened to his emotions, and sometimes I had to alert him that his actions or the voice tone he used, hurt me. When I asked him if he thought he needed to apologize, most of the time he would say yes. I would always be intrigued when he wasn't aware he needed to apologize, but it helped me to understand why our shouting matches always ended with, "I don't like your tone!" and, "But momma, I didn't have an attitude!"

As teachers often tell their young students to use their inside voices when they are in the classroom, I began to work with Raymond on his tone. Sometimes he communicated with me the way he talked to his friends. He had become really comfortable with me and didn't understand that his tone was disrespectful. There were times I would ask him a question, and he would answer "yep" instead of "yes." After a few times of getting by with this, he thought I was just like one of his friends.

I soon realized that a key contributor to our shouting matches was our inability to understand how the other communicated. I explained to Raymond that females and males communicate differently, and that women should be spoken to with a softer tone, *especially* his mother.

During our quest to communicate effectively, there were times of triumph and there were many times of uninvited emotional outburst. Whether Raymond instigated a negative reaction within me, or my negative reaction was prompted by other factors, I *most always* apologized first. I emphasize "most always" because by now you know, I was far from being a perfect parent. I wanted to be an example to him and teach him that parents aren't perfect.

I was determined that Raymond and I would one day be able to communicate effectively — no matter how long it took, and by any means necessary. There were many times I said, "Son forgive me I was wrong," before I heard, "Mom, I'm sorry, please forgive me." Any sign of pride that attempted to keep me from apologizing first, was quickly eradicated. My strong desire outweighed and overruled any thought that tried to stop me from pursuing peace in our home altogether.

ᔫᔫᔫ

As parents, we may feel we shouldn't apologize to our children, even when we are wrong. Although parents are the adults, parents can't afford to be prideful by thinking that apologizing to their children will cause them not to respect their authority.

By apologizing, it helps children see that parents are human and are not perfect, and are not some "godly entity" trying to rule over them. Children are not inferior or ignorant just because they are younger. Their need for being able to trust and respect their parents is just as important as the parents' need for their children to respect and obey them.

When the child feels wronged by the parent, be assured, the trust and respect has been damaged. Not apologizing, can build up resistance between the parent and the child because the child may become emotionally distant from the parent. This resistance makes it hard for the child to talk openly to the parent, even about small matters. Instinctively, the child may build more barriers to protect him/her from being hurt again, causing even more communication problems.

Perhaps my brother, Dale, would have advised me to handle my communication issues with my son a little differently. As a single parent raising one of his children, he made single parenting seem so easy.

Although Dale's son, Shawn, always seemed to be more disciplined than Raymond, I knew parenting, *period*, was far from being easy, whether with one parent in the home or two. I realized my brother's parenting style was probably quite different than mine, and that he had the same key ingredient that my father had — a masculine voice of authority.

Life Lesson #7

Apparently, there is no universal method of disciplining children. Some parents believe in spanking their children, while others would never dream of using this method. Some parents believe in time-outs, while others may believe taking away a child's privilege is the most effective way to change behavior.

When parenting methods are effective and consistent, parents become the voice of authority that will positively influence the lives of their children.

Chapter 8

୬

STRATEGIES
Divine Intervention

PARENTING IS BY far the toughest job I've ever had. One of my managers often told me I was very organized. She knew if she asked me to do a task, I would accomplish it with little or no supervision. My manager also knew, if I didn't understand something, I would definitely ask questions. She had no clue these abilities came from being a single parent.

Single parents can't afford to wait on someone else to fix their problems. If something is broken, usually a single parent quickly figures out how to get it fixed; therefore, I had no problem asking God for strategies. His "Divine Intervention" not only worked in situations as vast as helping Moses in the Bible part the Red Sea, but also something as small as getting my son to stop using all the clean towels.

Because we only had a few towels, one of Raymond's chores was to wash towels every three or four days. He had track practice almost every day, and would take a shower without focusing on how many clean towels were in the closet.

One night, after my evening routine of cooking dinner and doing housework, I opened the hall closet to reach for a towel. When I saw only one towel in the closet, my emotions were set off like an Olympic runner taking off at the sound of the gunshot at the beginning of a race.

"Raymond is definitely going to get a piece of my mind when he comes home! He has done this too many times, and I'm tired of it!" I angrily declared.

Raymond didn't come home until later that evening because Michael had taken him to his track meet out of town. Even though we were divorced, Michael and Raymond still communicated from time to time. By the time Raymond came home, I was relaxed because I had a chance to unwind. I also had time to re-think the situation, so I didn't pronounce a severe judgment on him. Typically, when I was tired, his consequences were based on the level of stress I experienced that day, rather than his actions.

I prayed and asked God to give me a strategy to encourage Raymond to stop using all the towels. I knew this was a small thing, but I also knew God cared about the small stuff, too. God knew this was important to me, not just because we were out of towels, but because He cared about me and my needs.

As usual, God answered my prayer. He impressed upon me to only put three or four towels in the closet and keep the rest out of Raymond's view; therefore, when Raymond used up all the towels, if he wanted clean ones, he could wash the towels he had used.

On most days, I always found something to nag Raymond about. His cluttered room was at the top of my list. Keeping his room clean was definitely not one of his priorities, so this was always a major issue.

When I asked him to clean his room, he would clean it using the "out of sight, out of my mother's mind" method. Raymond would move things from the top of the bed to underneath the bed, or off the floor and into the closet.

The issue with Raymond's room seemed to be never-ending. What he thought was clean I thought was half-clean. When he thought he had done a great job, to me, he had done a mediocre job. Because he never sufficiently cleaned his room to my satisfaction, whenever we discussed it, our conversation would end in a heated disagreement.

Because of my daily stresses during the week, I often found myself constantly nagging Raymond about *every* little thing. Sadly, he became the target for the release of my tension and frustration. I knew my unhealthy emotional reactions could have negative effects on him; therefore, I instigated "Whatever Days."

On "Whatever Days," I intentionally overlooked things that were minuscule, but could appear to be extreme due to the daily pressures of being a single parent. This strategy allowed my son to be himself without fear that I would nag him if he didn't live up to my expectations.

Life Lesson #8

It is vital for challenges to be addressed immediately in the single parent household. Recurring challenges steal time and energy, and also create stress.

When overwhelmed, parents may display unhealthy negative emotions at the slightest agitation. Parents can develop strategies to eliminate cyclical issues that cause stress in the home. Creating strategies can also help parents focus on their children's positive behavior, and increase compliments that will build their self-esteem.

Chapter 9

BECAUSE I SAID SO
Effective Communication

M Y PARENTS USED the phrase, "Because I said so," quite often. This phrase carried much weight and tremendous power. Without a doubt, this significant statement meant the conversation is over and not to be talked about again.

Unfortunately, I didn't use this statement enough. When Raymond was younger, I thought by allowing him to freely express himself, we would have a close relationship. Because he had excellent debating skills, which he used at the most inopportune times; giving him this freedom only caused a lot of tension and frustration.

Because I had the responsibility of both parents, the pressures of parenting often became so overwhelming, that a plethora of emotions would arouse in me, waiting to implode at any time. To make matters worse, somewhere along the way I also picked up the "never let them see you sweat" attitude, so I didn't talk much to others about my struggle. I tried to paint a picture on the outside to make others think that I had this "single parenting thing" down pat. But only

God knew that I was smiling on the outside, but really crying on the inside.

At times, the pain would be so excruciating that I would often tell Raymond, "One day, you are going to come home and find the doors locked, and I will be gone to Dallas!" But somehow God always miraculously intervened. God was well aware of the struggle we were going through. He didn't take the struggle from us, but He helped us through it—sometimes through a word of wisdom and encouragement from my close friends, at other times, through an expression on my son's face that seemed to say, "Momma, don't give up, I know you're hurting and scared, but I'm hurting and scared, also."

Sometimes when Raymond called home from a friend's house, I felt he was checking on me to make sure I hadn't packed up and ran away. I could tell in his voice that he actually believed he would come home one day and find the doors locked, and his mom no where to be found.

In a conversation with my cousin, Ollie, she curiously asked me, "When things are tough, why do you always run?"

After our conversation, I discovered that I was only trying to get away from the pain. I realized if running away from the pressure meant giving up my son, I needed to learn a different way to deal with the pressure.

One Sunday, I made an appointment with my realtor to look at houses after church. I told Raymond to ask our cousin, Darryl, if he could go home with him until I finished looking at houses. This was a simple request, but Raymond failed to comply, and waited to go find Darryl after church was over. When I told him it was too late, and I was ready to leave, he became upset and proclaimed that he didn't want to go with me to look at houses. As usual, his tone caused me to produce a cataclysmic emotional outburst.

We all know, as volcano eruptions do not give heed to time or surroundings, emotional outburst don't regard time or place either. Whether at home, in the mall, or parked in a church parking lot, if the temperature is elevated high enough, WARNING — an eruption is about to occur!

As we sat in my car in the parking lot, I angrily expressed my feelings to Raymond. After awhile, being tired of hearing me pontificating, he despondently interjected, "Okay mom, I understand."

By this time, I was on overkill. "You started this hell, so you're going to finish listening to it!" I shouted.

Even though Raymond was dead wrong, my reaction definitely was not right. Although there may have been many factors that caused my emotional outburst such as stress, unrealized expectations, or other underlying issues, these factors did not justify my reaction. I should have been more aware of my emotions and feelings, and not let my emotions rise to a level that could negatively affect my son's self-esteem and inevitably prolong the manifestation of his true potential.

After a volcanic eruption, there are different signs that signify an eruption has taken place. While the external evidence of a volcanic eruption is clearly visible, the effects underneath the surface must be scientifically viewed.

The evidence of the effects of an emotional outburst is no different. The external evidence is manifested openly in negative outward behavior, but the internal effects are not all easily seen by the human eye. During an emotional outburst, our core being is significantly altered, creating a rippling internal effect that damages self-esteem and inevitably creates more intense emotional reactions.

~·~·~

On most days during the week, I didn't have time to cook breakfast before I went to work. Saturday mornings were the times I cherished and enjoyed cooking because Raymond and I could eat and have quality time together.

Most of the time, I would prepare something light, like cream of wheat and toast. If I was really in a good mood, I would cook bacon and eggs, along with fried potatoes and onions. On occasion, I would make pancakes and add cherry topping and whip cream, hoping Raymond would always remember these times as a special family tradition.

As Raymond grew older, he often slept late on the weekends and sometimes didn't eat breakfast. I couldn't understand how he could pass up the pancakes I had cooked by using Aunt Mamie's homemade recipe. I figured sleeping late was his way of telling me he was bored with my homemade renditions of "International House of Pancake Specials," or maybe staying in bed on Saturdays was his favorite weekend thing.

Whenever I cooked pancakes, the solution to him sleeping late was quite simple. Since no one loved my pancakes more than I did, it really didn't matter that he didn't eat. Being the "leftover food queen," I put the leftovers in the refrigerator and ate them the next day. No harm. No foul.

On the other hand, the "Cream of Wheat and Toast Special" I cooked the following Saturday, didn't go over quite as well. I honestly believe, the unrealistic image of June Cleaver that was locked within my soul, over-powered me this particular morning. Although I didn't have an apron around my waist and my makeup and hair neatly in place, my expectation of Raymond and I eating together was still the same. Unfortunately, Ward Cleaver wasn't sitting in the chair in the living room reading the morning newspaper, nor was he close by to save me from the emotional display that was about to occur.

This particular morning I was really excited about cooking cream of wheat for breakfast. After cooking it for precisely five minutes, I added exactly three teaspoons of sugar and a touch of butter to bring out the perfect flavor. Because you can't save cream of wheat for leftovers (at least I hadn't found a way), it *must* be eaten while it's piping hot.

As I began to tear small pieces of toast to put in the bowl of cream of wheat (for no longer than 6.5 seconds of course, so it won't get too mushy), I called for Raymond to come and eat. However, he decided to sleep late again, missing out on our special Saturday morning ritual.

As I sat alone at the table eating my cream of wheat and watching Raymond's bowl out of the corner of my eyes, my emotions began to stir and my emotional temperature began to rise. This was a clear warning sign that the little volcano inside of me was about to erupt. "Oh, no!" I thought to myself. "I *must* control my emotions, I *can* do this!" But as I tried to enjoy my own bowl of cream of wheat, I found myself on edge, and I took one more glance at Raymond's bowl, which by now had turnéd to gel.

Evidently, my expectation of Raymond eating breakfast with me was not that important to him. I stormed in his room and lectured him about not eating the bowl of cream of wheat I had so passionately cooked. But to my surprise, Raymond listened quietly without interrupting. When I finished, he calmly responded, "Okay mom, I understand." He then, put the covers over his head, and went back to sleep.

I slowly walked out of Raymond's room feeling ashamed that I allowed a bowl of cream of wheat to affect my emotions. To remind me that I let something so small have victory over me and control my behavior, I put the empty box of cream of wheat on top of the fire place for a week.

As usual, I apologized to Raymond. I decided the next time I cook breakfast, I would ask him the night before if he wanted the "Pancake Special," "Cream of Wheat Special," or "Let Me Sleep Late Special."

·෴·෴·෴

Our environment is never constant. We are always growing and always changing; therefore, our emotional response is usually subjective and based on many variables. Because of these factors, the length of time the process takes to modify and change behavior is not categorical.

I began to consider my quest for peace, a "work in progress." As restaurants being renovated often display signs that state: "Please excuse our mess, we are under construction to better serve you." Whenever my conversation with Raymond ended in disharmony, I wanted to wear a tee shirt that stated: "Please excuse our mess. We are creating loving behavior to better serve each other."

As I sat at the table talking with Raymond one evening about school, I sensed a shouting match was starting to brew. We both tried to get our point across, but our display of emotional frustration and anger kept getting in the way. As in most cases, the discussion could have been finished quickly, but our lack of communication skills interfered with our ability to stay focused on the topic at hand.

I asked Raymond if he loved me, and he said yes. I also asked him if he intentionally wanted to hurt me, and he said no. I told him that I loved him and I didn't want to hurt him either. I explained to Raymond that over the years we had been communicating with each other out of our pain, and it would take time to learn how to communicate based on our love for each other.

I was always excited to try different methods to enhance our communication skills. I'm sure "Divine Intervention" led me to question Raymond about his love for me. Because I knew we both loved each other, I was even more excited to continue my pursuit of finding the root cause that hindered our ability to communicate in a loving manner.

While Raymond and I continued to talk, I looked across the table and saw a ruler on top of his notebook. So, I picked up the ruler and stated, "Raymond, when I am holding the ruler, it's my turn to talk. When you are holding the ruler, it's your turn to talk."

After using this approach, surprisingly, our conversation ended peacefully. Raymond and I learned a strategy to help control our emotions, and as a result this strategy also helped us to respect each other's thoughts and feelings.

I decided to use the newly established "ruler method" each time we talked about a serious issue. Although Raymond and I loved and cared for each other, it was clear that we had a difficult time showing it because of our emotions. Most of the time, the anger we expressed was not related to the issue we were discussing. The stress and frustration we encountered each day was targeted at the person we loved the most, each other.

∽∽∽

There may be parents that disagree with the "ruler method," but this strategy was very beneficial in helping us on our quest to restore peace in our home. I am in no way saying children should speak their mind at anytime, or that parents should always give their children an explanation of their decisions.

Sometimes parents fail to realize that their children's negative behavior stems from the parents' actions. Without this knowledge, parents often expect their children to have the answer to why they behaved a certain way, and automatically expect them to know how to fix themselves.

Although I strongly believe that children should obey their parents, I must also express that it is equally important for parents to accept the responsibility of fixing what is broken in their homes.

In order to communicate effectively, Raymond and I had to learn how to control our emotions and modify our reactions. In some instances, I took the time to explain a situation to him in order for him to learn a life lesson. But whenever he acted disrespectfully and began to question a decision I made, I learned to quickly interject, "Because I said so!

Life Lesson #9

Unhealthy emotional reactions are indeed "weapons of mass destruction." When parents communicate with their children using these destructive emotions, it often creates challenges for them to function as healthy, responsible adults.

As parents provide the basic necessities of clothes and food to feed their children, it is also imperative that parents find ways to effectively communicate with their children in order to protect and preserve their self-esteem.

Chapter 10

✒

INSTRUCTIONS NOT INCLUDED
Acquiring Knowledge

D R. WOO HAD been my doctor for over fifteen years. Because my exams and consultations were always thorough, she was familiar with my different stages of growth and development, as well as the stressful life events that caused my blood pressure to rise.

It was always important to me that I left the doctor's office more knowledgeable than when I arrived. Sometimes I would get caught up in Dr. Woo's animated way of explaining things that I would forget to ask questions. So, before each visit, I always wrote out my questions and concerns.

My doctor's appointment was scheduled during my lunch hour. Once I was checked into the exam room, I waited over twenty minutes before the nurse came in and did her usual routine. My weight, temperature, and blood pressure were all normal. She flipped the switch on the outer door to alert the doctor that I was ready for her, and expressed with a smile, "The doctor will be in shortly."

What was supposed to be a few minutes, turned into thirty minutes, and thirty minutes turned into an hour. But since I wasn't in any hurry to get back to work, I decided to take advantage of the time away from my dollhouse size cubicle.

To pass the time, I used my cell phone to call my friend, Robert, who lived in Dallas. I chatted and laughed freely even though the clock on the wall was ticking fast, and I was definitely going to be late getting back to work.

Finally, the doctor knocked on the door and proceeded to come in. With her bigger than life smile, she said hello and reached out to shake my hand. "So, Benita, how's life treating you?"

Dr. Woo never failed to ask the same question at the beginning of every visit. She knew my physical and emotional history very well, so I casually responded, assuming my response to her question would inform her if I was living a balanced life.

After Dr. Woo completed my exam, she stated with excitement: "No apparent signs of illness or stress. The last time you were here you expressed that your job was stressful. I'm glad you took my advice and learned how to deal with your stress. You're in great health. That's wonderful!"

As she began to write up the paperwork for my blood tests, I began to ask her one hundred and one questions.

"I know you've told me this before, but can you tell me what causes high blood pressure?"

This time was no different than any other. With a big smile on her face, she began to give me a history lesson.

"How did your people get over here?"

"On a boat," I cautiously answered as though I was taking a history test. I thought it was quite intriguing that my Asian doctor was giving *me*, an African American, a lesson about my ancestors, during my physical exam.

Dr. Woo eagerly continued her explanation: "When your ancestors were brought over here they were jammed together. The more people the slave owners could fit on the boat, the more money they would receive. Because the conditions were horrendous, many people died from dehydration.

The people that were able to retain the water, survived. Even though it was good that your ancestors could retain water, once they came over here, they ate more salt, and the salt caused their pressure to go up and their heart to pump faster."

"If you look at the genetic aspect of things," she enthusiastically added, "you will be able to better understand how your body works and how to make it function properly. Each of us has inherent pre-existing traits that have been passed down from generation to generation. If you know what the traits are and how they affect you, you can take precautionary measures that will enable you to live a long and healthy life."

After my exam, I left the doctor's office excited about the knowledge I had gained. I had a choice to either follow my doctor's advice on living a healthy life, or try to stay healthy by my own limited knowledge. Without her guidance I knew my health was sure to suffer, so I was determined to follow her exact instructions.

◦◦◦◦

"Raising a child doesn't come with an instruction manual," was a statement I heard my friend say when she was going through a difficult period of child rearing. But I beg to differ.

After my visit to the doctor's office, I realized that parents *can* learn to raise their children to become healthy, responsible adults. Just as there are a wide variety of books on medical information, there are also many instruction manuals available for parents to gain wisdom and knowledge on parenting. The question is: *Are parents willing to search for the knowledge, and then, apply it?*

Without utilizing the knowledge that is available, our children suffer. When parents do not take the time to equip themselves on effective parenting, the cost of not acquiring this knowledge is great, and our children pay a hefty price.

As parents, our focus *has* to change. We can no longer use the excuse that our parents weren't perfect, and we aren't perfect either. Parents are not perfect and never will be, but this truth should not be an excuse to casually prepare our children for adulthood. While television shows survive on ratings, actors receive Academy Awards, and cars are rated by performance, should we as parents be let off the hook?

Please don't misconstrue my intentions. I'm not pointing fingers or casting blame, but could it be possible that as the Purslane flower closes when the sun goes down, we as parents have closed our eyes to the problems our children are facing?

As parents, we must painstakingly make every effort to equip our children and prepare them for their future. As Hansel and Gretel dropped bread crumbs to guide them back home, the wisdom and knowledge we impart to our children will also guide and instruct them along their path in life.

Again, I must beg to differ. "Instructions *Are* Included." We must find them, read them, and then, choose to follow the directions precisely.

Life Lesson #10

It is not by happenstance that children aren't considered adults until they are eighteen—preparing them to become healthy, responsible adults, doesn't happen over night.

"Parenting with purpose" helps parents to focus on empowering their children with the tools needed to succeed in life. When parents are not naturally equipped to impart these tools, acquiring this knowledge should be a priority.

Chapter 11

✒

TOUGH LOVE
R-E-S-P-E-C-T

I HAD OFTEN heard about this thing called "tough love," it sounded like an old cliché to me, only something you read in books, or a phrase you heard in a therapist's office. I casually put that phrase in the back of my mind like tucking away a twenty dollar bill deep in your wallet, only to be used for a rainy day.

Although Raymond and I continued to make great strides in our quest to communicate effectively, he still displayed signs of being in pain from missing his father. He rampantly journeyed through his teenage years like a vampire on the hunt for blood on the night of a full moon! I had finally reached the breaking point, and I didn't need anyone's advice on how to get that boy back in line. I reached back in time and pulled out the information on "tough love" that I had neatly tucked away in the back of my mind, and proceeded to try anything and everything that would put an end to this tumultuous season in our lives.

Raymond often displayed the "I need my daddy to tell me who I am" syndrome, and his attitude undeniably stated, "I'm almost grown and I wanna do what I please!"

As a car that just lost control, Raymond's actions were

clearly screaming, "Somebody, help me! I've lost control and I can't stop this madness!"

Raymond often proclaimed that once he was grown he was going to leave home.

"I'm getting out of here when I get eighteen!" he would angrily shout.

"You don't have to wait until you are eighteen! Why don't you leave now?" I would shout back.

"After everything I've done for him, he chooses to act like *this*? This boy must be crazy!" I thought to myself. "You would think he'd be grateful!"

But oh, no! Raymond was in agony over so many things; mainly, his dad not being around. The only way he knew how to express his feelings, undoubtedly, was to hurt me. I realized his actions were predicated by his yearning for his father, and his pain did not acquiesce to logic or reason. I could see the anguish on in his face whenever I talked to him about his father. His eyes would scrunch up, and lines would pop-up on his forehead like birds flying in formation.

Although Raymond never cried, within my heart I knew my son was still suffering, and perhaps that is why I didn't give up on him. He didn't know that his momma was about to lose her ehva-lovin' mind because of his rebellious behavior. I knew this was something I had to walk through, or should I say, pray through. I couldn't turn my back on my son in the midst of his pain. I had to be strong and hold it all together if we were both going to survive and still have any dignity left.

∽∽∽∽

It seemed no matter what I did for Raymond, he would still have a callous attitude as though he had something to prove. The look of anger, pain, and disillusionment on his face was my signal that he preferred to be left alone.

I see this same look on the faces of many young boys everywhere. Because "pain is pain," it also affects young girls who get mixed up with so called "bad boys" because they are looking for the male authority they didn't have growing up. Sadly, these "bad boys" become father figures and take the place of the fathers who weren't around for their baby girls. But that's a whole different book!

Women undeniably stand in the gap for their children's fathers, and unfortunately, instead of honoring them, society has labeled them. Let's face it, we *have* to be strong in order for our families to survive, but deep within our hearts, we desire that men be the fathers they were created to be.

❧❧❧

As though his angry attitude was his personal security blanket, Raymond continued to walk around with a chip on his shoulder. I will admit, I gave him an abundance of mercy, but when he flat out did wrong, I gave him consequences for his actions. Each time the "tough love" I implemented didn't work; I increased the level of punishment and set more boundaries, hoping this would change his behavior. It seemed hard for him to get passed his pain, but I knew it was crucial he understood that even though he was angry his father was not around, his negative behavior was unacceptable.

There were times Raymond understood my perspective about a situation, thought about the choice he had made, and adjusted his actions. Like the time he claimed he found a cell phone at a party and decided to keep it. I didn't think much about it until one day Raymond called me from an unrecognizable number. He had a job, so I figured he bought a new cell phone. After a few days, I needed to ask him a question, so I dialed the number that had appeared on my phone from his previous call. And, I was shocked when I heard a girl's voice on the recording!

"Hi, my name is Angela. I lost my cell phone. If you find it, please call me at xxx-xxxx."

I could not believe my ears. "What is Raymond thinking?" I asked myself.

When he came home, I asked him about the message on the phone. He claimed he found the phone at a party, so he felt he should be able to keep it. I collected myself before speaking to make sure I didn't over react (*this came from practice*), hoping Raymond would think about what he just said.

"Raymond, if you really believe that and think that's fair, are you saying, if someone found the keys to your car it would belong to them?"

Giving him something to ponder, I left the room and didn't bring the subject back up.

Later that evening, I asked Junior, my nephew who was visiting with us, where Raymond had gone. He said Raymond left to take the girl her cell phone.

"Wow! If Raymond could think through his problems this easily every time, our journey through life would be so much smoother," I thought, with a smile on my face. (*But maybe then, I wouldn't be writing this book*).

◦◦◦◦

When I came home from work one evening, Raymond and Junior were watching television. We had moved into another apartment complex to be closer to his school. I had planned to buy a new home in six months, so to save money I only leased a one bedroom apartment. Once again, I gave Raymond the bedroom.

Later that evening, as I walked past Raymond's room, I noticed a sheet nailed up to the window. Although it slightly upset me, I didn't ask him any questions. I continued on to the bathroom to wash my hands, and while throwing the paper towel away, I saw an empty condom wrapper in the trash can.

The Fourth of July came early that year! My emotions were set off and I was downright enraged! I ranted and raved so, you would have thought we were having the annual fireworks show right in the middle of our living room!

Although Raymond insisted the condom belonged to one of his friends, I exploded! But quite frankly, it really didn't matter to me who the condom belonged to. I wanted him to know that I was *crazy mad*!

"If you can't respect our home, you don't need any company! I can't believe you had the audacity to let one of your friends have sex in our home while I was at work!" I shouted.

I was angry, hurt, and embarrassed because Junior saw me fly off the handle. Immediately, I told him to pack his bags so I could take him home.

"And furthermore," I angrily shouted, "we'll talk about your consequences when we get back from taking Junior home!"

Because Raymond was a good talker, he could debate his way out of anything. He could present his case as though he graduated magna cum laude from Harvard Law School. Most of the time he had a convincing explanation, but at other times, I was just plain tired and overlooked his actions. But now I was furious, and I was determined to overrule any justification, no matter how compelling he presented his case!

After a long day at work, and finally arriving back home from dropping Junior off, a two hour drive I hadn't planned, Raymond and I talked about the consequences for his actions. I didn't give him a chance to tell his side of the story. I gave him my usual lecture, and then, informed him that since he thought he was grown enough to do what he pleased in my home, he would now have to pay rent each month. I never believed his story about the condom belonging to his friend, but since I couldn't prove it, I decided to settle for rent.

·҂·҂·҂

I knew Raymond wasn't perfect and would make mistakes, but when he was downright disrespectful, I would definitely protect my right to be respected and immediately become outraged! "My job is paying the bills and your job is paying respect!" I would shout intensely.

During his teenage years, I often insisted he leave the house when he was disrespectful. Usually, he stayed with one of his friends overnight. But one summer his behavior was so uncontrollable, I made him leave home, and he spent the whole summer with his friend, Jay, and his parents.

At times, I put Raymond out because I was overwhelmed and hadn't learned how to deal with my stress. Once when I told him to leave, he replied, "Momma, I don't want to leave. I don't have an attitude. Whatever I did, I'm sorry!"

I was really glad he apologized *first* this time, because I didn't want him to leave either. I had always envisioned my son leaving home when he went to college, not being put out of the house because he had done something wrong, or because I over reacted.

·҂·҂·҂

Like Oklahoma weather, the atmosphere in our home could change drastically without warning. It seemed, not a week went by that we had consistent peace. If Raymond spoke to me in the wrong voice tone, I would inevitably lose control of my emotions and the rollercoaster ride would begin.

Raymond's attitude had been horrible all week, so I declared enough was enough. But this time, when I told him to leave, he only ignored me. In that moment, compelled by anger and frustration, I called the very authority that I was determined to protect my son from, the police.

When the police arrived, I explained the situation to them. They talked to Raymond and told him that he should want to respect me because I was his mother and had made many sacrifices for him.

Before they left, one policeman told me that my son was really a good kid. I could tell he thought "our problem" was not a "real problem" at all.

"Lady, there are many parents dealing with kids who are in gangs and on drugs who would love to have your problem," he sincerely stated.

After the police left, Raymond apologized as though he truly understood the ramifications of being disrespectful.

Life Lesson #11

When seeking to change behavior, discipline should be used in conjunction with love. The end result of discipline should be a lesson learned that can be used for a lifetime. Likewise, the end result of love should give our children reassurance in knowing, even in discipline, our love for them is unwavering.

Chapter 12

✣

NO! MEANS NO!
Say What You Mean and Mean What You Say

A LTHOUGH RAYMOND AND I continued to work on our communication skills; from time to time our lives still exhibited the effects of our inner pain. Even though we didn't always discuss our problems peacefully, I didn't allow my emotional flare-ups to interfere with the excitement of buying a new home.

During the process of looking at houses, my rental property became vacant. My mother had previously lived in my rental property, and decided to move next door.

As I prepared to fix up the house to rent it again, I hired Paul to do the repairs. My mother had introduced me to Paul and was pleased with the work he completed for her, so I didn't question his work ethics or his work performance.

Because the house was vacant, I gave Paul a key. This saved me time from meeting him to unlock the door before I went to work and then, going back to the house again to lock the door after he left for the day.

Sometimes when I went by the house on my lunch break to check his progress, I would find liquor bottles in the trash can. The work would be done, but the "clean as you go" principle was definitely not first on Paul's priority list.

It was evident Paul could do great work, but his drinking definitely interfered with his ability to keep his personal and professional life separate. Unfortunately, Paul's drinking was just the beginning of the manifestations of his internal struggles.

Each week there was a different episode with Paul that was more interesting than any daytime soap opera. My mother informed me that Paul had separated from his wife, Rebekah, who was six months pregnant. To my surprise, Paul told his wife that we were living together in my rental property.

I was terrified that one day Rebekah would decide to come and investigate for herself, and furiously demand I leave her husband alone if she found this to be true. By this time, Paul had completed with the first phase of putting texture on the walls. Because of his negligence, he put texture on the crown molding and the floors, too.

I was relieved when my mother told me she had taken Rebekah to the house to show her it was empty, and that it was not possible for anyone to be living there. Evidently, after seeing the condition of the house for herself, Rebekah must have logically concluded that her husband's statement about the two of us was prompted by his drinking, and was quite far from the truth. Fortunately, she decided not to drag me into their marital problems and never talked to me about the matter. After my two marriages, Lord knows, relationship drama was the last thing I needed.

I guess the signs were not clear enough for me to see that I needed to fire Paul. The drinking and the lies he had told about us living together, apparently were not enough. Because I didn't like confrontation, I let him stick around for another dramatic episode before I came to my senses.

᪥᪥᪥

As Paul continued to work, I began to wonder if he was from a single parent household that did not provide him with clear boundaries. I am not suggesting there is a lack of discipline in every single parent home, nor am I pointing the finger at any parent. But I will be the first to admit that sometimes I did fail to implement consequences to my son for unacceptable behavior.

How many times do parents tell their children "no," but after they whine or throw a fit, change the decision to "yes" because the children have gotten on the parent's nerves?

How many times do parents threaten their children by saying, "You better not run through this house again, or I'm going to spank you!" Or repeatedly ask the question, "Do you want me to get my belt?"

Parents may repeat these statements time-and-time again before they take any action, and most often, never take any action at all to discipline their children. Sadly, children see these statements as idle threats. They tune out their parents and continue with their unruly behavior.

I am not by any means a Doctor or Psychologist, but I am quite sure there are many reasons adults have made unwise choices that have caused them to be incarcerated. Whatever the reason, I propose, the root cause stemmed from unresolved issues, unclear boundaries, or a lack of discipline for unacceptable behavior while growing up.

At the risk of being ridiculed, I make these points to illustrate the connection between unresolved childhood issues and negative adult behavior. Again, I am not placing blame on any parent, but if the words I write help prevent one mother's son or daughter from going to prison, and save one son or daughter's mother from shedding tears, I *must* absolutely put myself on the line.

~~*~~

Although I naively continued to let Paul work; I knew it would only be a matter of time before I would have to let him go. Each day, as his mother continued to drop off her forty year old son to work on my rental property, it became more apparent to me that his adult behavior was indicative of not receiving consequences for his actions as a child.

Paul worked diligently for the next two weeks. But when he left the front door open all night, I finally made up my mind to fire him.

Once I calculated the cost to finish the repairs, I realized it was going to take a great deal of time and money before I could rent the house to someone again. My apartment lease was up in one month, so reluctantly, I decided to move back into the house and take my time to complete the work.

Raymond and I began to clean up the mess Paul had left behind. During this time, because the news media showed continuous coverage of 9-11 and talked about the negative effects the tragedy would have on the economy, I felt moving back into the house was probably a wise idea after all.

After we finished getting the house in order, Raymond's friend, Jay, helped us paint. All the while, I never told Raymond that we were going to move back into the house. It had always been my desire to provide a home for him in an upscale neighborhood. Moving back into our old house didn't make me feel warm and fuzzy inside, so I prolonged telling him the truth for as long as I could.

A few weeks later, Paul called and informed me that he was ready to start the next phase. Without any hesitation, I let him know that I no longer needed his help.

"Are you sure? Don't you want me to finish the job?" he asked, as if he had no idea why I let him go.

"No, Paul, I no longer need your services," I responded.

"But what are you going to do about the painting? Are you sure you don't want my help?"

"Paul, my son and I will clean up and do the painting! I emphatically stated, hoping he would get the message this time. But of course, he didn't. As he began to speak again, I abruptly interrupted him and unequivocally stated, "Paul, NO! MEANS NO!"

Life Lesson #12

Parents, when communicating to our children, we must explicitly say what we mean and mean what we say! When we vacillate back and forth in our decisions, this opens the door for our children to test our resolve.

The behavior children demonstrate and the choices they make will ultimately affect their future; therefore, parents must be steadfast in communicating clear boundaries, implementing discipline, and applying the appropriate consequences to unacceptable behavior. Without establishing boundaries, children make up their own rules based on their level of comprehension and reasoning. Boundaries also keep children safe and help parents gage their growth and maturity.

Chapter 13

☙

YOURS, MINE, AND NOT OURS
The Value of Money

GROWING UP THE youngest of five children, I never questioned if I was rich or poor. With my mother being a natural homemaker, and from what I saw as my "bring home the bacon, never without a job" father, this picture provided a good balance of parenting for me. Although there were financial challenges, I can never recall a time we went hungry or were ever voted the worst dressed at school. Our parents, raised during the Depression, somehow kept their sense of pride and instilled in us a high sense of self-esteem over providing the latest style of fashion.

As a single parent, there were plenty of times my son and I did without things we desired, but I never measured our self-worth by material things. I always knew our self-worth was more precious than rubies, more valuable than gold, and worth more than money could ever buy. I also believed that true riches came from within, so no amount of lack and no degree of pain could keep us down. Without a doubt, I was confident our inner riches would sustain us through the hard times.

☙☙☙

When Raymond was younger, buying his clothes was always easy because he didn't seem to care what I picked out for him. But as he grew older, he developed his own sense of style. His taste became more elaborate as the television commercials portrayed the flamboyant fashions.

Occasionally, I would buy Raymond an expensive shirt. I felt we had gone without buying luxuries for so long, treating him every once in a while seemed harmless. However, Raymond saw this as an opportunity to ask for more, as if I could blink my eyes and money would appear out of nowhere.

Unaware of the ramifications, I continued to buy Raymond the clothes he desired. His expectations continually increased, while my income was definitely not keeping up with his expectations. Eventually, Raymond reached a point where he only wanted to wear a certain brand of clothing. Like Dorothy following the "yellow brick road" on the Wizard of Oz, trying to get back to Kansas, I followed the red "on sale" signs searching for discount prices. (*In reality, the clothes I bought on sale weren't bargains at all because they were priced too high in the first place*).

Although I liked Raymond's sense of style, after a few years, I began to despise his style as well as his unappreciative attitude. He had developed a mindset that he should always be able to get what he wanted, despite the cost. Knowing that outward appearances don't always reflect the true inward attitude, I knew I had to make a change, and fast.

Without realizing it, I was locked in a warped mindset: part guilt and part ignorance. Guilt, because I wanted Raymond to see that despite our hardships, we were still blessed; and ignorance, because I didn't realize the effects of allowing him to continue in the mindset of wanting a certain style of clothes. Unfortunately, it took me a while to learn that the only flavor these two ingredients created was: DISASTER.

To make matters worse, Raymond's perspective was that all the kids were wearing expensive tennis shoes named after professional athletes, and he should have a pair, too. So, unwisely, I bought him a pair, then another, and another.

Raymond's father was also a part of the guilt-ignorance epidemic, having no clue of how buying his son high-priced shoes negatively influenced his mindset. Sometimes he would send Raymond an expensive pair of tennis shoes for Christmas or his birthday. Naturally, this won points with Raymond. Sadly, this was Raymond's special connection to his father, so how could I tell his father to stop sending these costly shoes, or not allow Raymond to wear them.

What makes children think just because they wear tennis shoes named after a professional athlete, they automatically attain the athlete's status of success without little or no effort? To make matters even worse, what causes parent's to fall into the trap of buying these shoes for their children? The answer to that question is still the same, "guilt and ignorance," and yes, that's my final answer.

The real truth of the matter is that children develop a false sense of self-worth when parents continuously pay outrageous prices for their children's clothes and shoes. When children work and want to spend their own money on expensive items, teaching them how to budget and save their money will help them be more conscious of the things they choose to buy.

When children are not taught the value of money, they often develop a mindset that is based on pleasurable spending. Believing expensive clothes are for any occasion, they feel they should be able to purchase these items at anytime, for any cost, and in every color.

While we were growing up, my siblings and I didn't wear expensive tennis shoes, and we didn't have a bad attitude as though the world owed us anything either; and you can bet your last dollar, our self-esteem is still in tact.

·෴·

Raymond had been driving the car he previously bought from his grandmother for almost two years before it finally stopped running. When he failed to make sure the car always had an adequate amount of oil in it, the motor locked up, and I became his convenient taxi driver.

After I became overwhelmed from taking Raymond to school, work, and his sports activities, I developed a plan for him to buy another car. I agreed to help him buy a car by contributing a certain amount of money based on his grades, and he agreed to continue to maintain a "B" average after he purchased the car. (*Good plan, I thought*).

Raymond worked hard to keep up his end of the deal. He maintained a "B" average the first semester of his junior year, and was diligent at working and saving his money. At the end of the second semester, Raymond was still on the honor roll and still saving money as planned, so I was excited to begin looking for him a car.

The car I found was a teal blue, Chevy Calvalier, which was definitely not Raymond's favorite color. Even though he didn't have all the money to pay for the car, I made him a small loan to cover the difference. I then, helped him prepare a budget so he could pay me back twenty-five dollars every pay check. This too, would have been a perfect plan, but I was not prepared for the challenges that were up ahead.

·෴·

I was overjoyed when Raymond became a senior. I was so excited, that I was oblivious to the warning signs that were flashing almost daily. Although these signs were right in front of me, regrettably, I missed them altogether.

For one, Raymond's school called me one day and asked

why he missed sixth hour. "Your guess is as good as mine," I responded in total amazement. Then, I found several parking tickets in his room for parking in the "no parking" zones at school. These little hints were the road signs I obviously overlooked, possibly thinking they would magically disappear without any serious action on my part, or any change in his behavior.

Whenever I talked to Raymond about his actions, he would somehow weasel his way out of the consequence he should have received. (*I plead guilty—I take full responsibility. I can say I was too tired, or too exhausted from work, but there was no excuse for not giving him consequences for his actions*).

Raymond also started getting tickets for speeding and running red lights. Because of my fear of him being stopped by the police, I would go against logic and loan him the money to pay the tickets. Needless to say, he didn't put forth any effort to change his behavior because he knew "his mom" would jump right in and pay them. One year, because he had lost his job, instead of buying him a birthday and Christmas gift, I paid his car insurance and one of his outstanding tickets. (*I know, somebody should have taken away my parenting license*). I should have prohibited him from driving when these issues first occurred in high school, but my need and desperation for him to have his own transportation overrode my judgment.

~·~·~

When Raymond graduated, he decided to postpone going to college for a few years to work and save money. Although this was not my ideal plan for him, I figured I could recoup some of the money he owed me, so I agreed.

Raymond worked several different jobs his first year out of high school. He would stay on his budget for two months or so, and then, out of nowhere, quit his job and be off work for several months. In the mean time, I would pick up the slack by loaning him money to buy gas so he could look for another job. (*I know, go ahead; put me in the corner*).

As I saw Raymond's habit of quitting a job at the drop of a hat and expecting me to pick up the pieces, I realized he needed to take responsibility for his actions. I knew his behavior was not going to change as long as I bailed him out, so I decided to break his habit of thinking that I was his twenty-four hour ATM.

After awhile, whenever he asked for money, I would tell him I didn't have any. He would then say, "But momma, you work, so I know *we* got money." (*Oh, no, he didn't! What does he mean, we got money!*)

When he continued to persist and ask me for money, I would always say the same thing, "I don't have any money!"

Finally, one day the light bulb came on. I didn't feel right about what I was saying, because after all, I worked everyday, I was on a budget, and I *did* have money. "Whenever I go out to lunch, I only eat half of my meal and save the rest for dinner," I thought to myself. "*I'm* the one sacrificing!"

"It's not that I don't have any money! Raymond doesn't have any money, and it's about time *somebody* told him that!" I spoke loudly to myself, trying to build up the courage to confront him.

Finally, after I pumped myself up, I decided to break the news to Raymond. For once and for all, he needed to know the real truth about *my* money.

"Son, I need to talk to you about something," I stated.

Raymond never failed to ask the same question whenever I told him that I needed to talk with him.

"Is it good or is it bad?" he asked anxiously.

"It's about you always asking me for money," I responded curtly. "You seem to...," and before I could finish my sentence, Raymond interrupted me and stated: "Oh, my gosh! What is it now?"

"Raymond, you seem to have a bad habit of asking me for money. You are a grown man now and are responsible for your own needs. I go to work eight hours everyday, even when I don't want to. I sacrifice and do without the luxuries that are not in my budget. If I do buy something, more than likely, it's on sale!" I expressed explicitly.

"I am the one that has money and you don't! The money I work hard for is mine! What you work hard for is yours! So, please let this be your final notice: *When it comes to money, there is no such thing as ours!"*

Life Lesson #13

Children are taught the value of money when they work for the things they desire. By working, their understanding of the value of money increases, which helps to build a solid financial foundation.

Hard work also instills in children a sense of pride and confidence. As they sacrifice and plan to reach their financial goals, a strong determination and self-discipline is established.

Chapter 14

◈

THE GRANDMOTHER NEXT DOOR
Wisdom, Support, and Peach Cobbler

I CAN CLEARLY remember when Raymond was six weeks old. All I wanted for my birthday was to get a full night's sleep. He hadn't slept all night since he was born, and I was extremely exhausted. I would have given anything in those days for eight hours of uninterrupted sleep—no bottles, no crying—just me and my pillow and the sweet sound of absolute peace and quiet.

I asked momma if she would watch Raymond all night as my birthday gift, instead of giving me a dress, jewelry, or any amount of cash for that matter. But her response was a flat, "No!" No explanation. No hesitation. Not even a bit of sympathy.

I figured this was her way of letting me know that Raymond was *my* responsibility come hell or high water, and that I would have to put his needs before my own, even if it meant functioning on little or no sleep at all.

Momma even expected me to have his bottle ready before he woke up crying from his nap. "You should have already had his bottle prepared. You knew he was going to be hungry when he woke up!" she would say, in her outspoken manner of getting her point across.

Momma was close by from the beginning. Before I knew Raymond was even coming into this world, she knew long before I did that the stork was about to make a special delivery.

My husband and I lived across the street from her. Almost daily for two months, I would go to her house and swipe her pickles. "Boy these pickles are always so good," I thought to myself. "I just can't seem to get enough of them."

Momma never said a word, so I didn't think she was paying me any mind, or even realized her pickles were disappearing each day.

It wasn't until I went to the doctor because of a ruptured cyst on my ovaries that I learned I was expecting. The doctor asked me if I was pregnant, and I told him without any reservation, "No, I'm definitely not!"

I guess he had heard this before and decided to do a pregnancy test anyway, just in case. I figured the results of the test would determine what type of anesthesia to use for my surgery.

The next day when the doctor's office called and told me the results were positive, I cried like a baby. I wanted to have a lot of children some day, but not until two or three years down the road, and definitely not so soon after I had gotten married.

When I told momma the news, she informed me she already knew. "Oh, I knew you were pregnant when my pickle jar kept coming up empty, and it wasn't me eating the pickles!" she stated, with a grin on her face.

·⁓⁓·⁓·⁓

My husband and I had separated before it was time to attend the childbirth class. Momma told me I had to still be strong for the baby, so even though I was afraid, I went to the childbirth class alone.

After I watched the video of the women giving birth, I rushed to momma's house crying hysterically. I told her that I didn't want to have the baby because the pain the women displayed in the film while they were going through labor, frightened me.

Although momma comforted me by letting me know everything was going to be alright, she also made me face reality real quick. "Seven months into the pregnancy is a little late to be afraid," she stated candidly.

One month later when my water broke, momma rushed me to the hospital. She made sure I was settled in my room, but once my friend, Paula, arrived, she left as fast as lightning. Some things momma just didn't do, and being in the room with a terrified mother about to give birth, was one of them!

Paula and I played Backgammon, so I wouldn't focus on the other women in labor that were expressing their pain. The nurse later gave me some medicine to help start my contractions, but twelve hours later, still no baby. Little Raymond was definitely taking his sweet time.

The next morning the doctor prepared me for a Cesarean section. He explained that my back was not strong enough to have a normal delivery, and he already planned for me to have a Cesarean birth. (*Why didn't he tell me this before now? It sure would have saved me from a lot of stress. Ya think?*)

A few hours later, my little bundle of joy was born. Because Raymond was premature, he only weighed a little over five pounds and had to stay in the incubator the majority of the time I was in the hospital. He wore a bright orange knitted cap to keep him warm, and momma held his tiny little fingers through the opening in the incubator.

When I brought Raymond home from the hospital, momma gave him his first bath. I watched attentively, hoping that one day I would be able to care for him as naturally as she did.

I'm sure momma could tell I was afraid of having the responsibility of caring for a baby on my own. Because Raymond's father was not around to help, I depended on her to be there for his first doctor's visit, and to answer many "Momma, how do I do this?" questions.

⁓⁓⁓

When Raymond grew older, momma took him to school with her while I was at work. She was a preschool teacher with a background in the Montessori Method of teaching. She often told me about a child's emotional needs, and explained how the child is negatively affected if their emotional needs were not met. Momma didn't only focus on Raymond as her grandson, but made sure I knew if he was lacking in any areas based on her knowledge and education.

Over the years, Raymond spent many weekends with his grandmother so I could have a break. Sometimes she took him with her to the Flea-Market where she sold antiques. While watching her, he learned a great deal about business as she negotiated prices with the customers.

Raymond had a "special thing" for his grandmother. They developed a bond that was tougher than superglue. I knew they both loved and cared for each other, so I didn't try to set any boundaries for their relationship, or influence him to establish the kind of relationship I would prefer them to have.

Whatever Raymond could not talk to me about, he shared with his grandmother. Some things I would have preferred he kept between the two of us, but usually she was his only outlet, so I accepted their close-knit bond.

Raymond would often run to his grandmother if I didn't approve of something he wanted to do, and usually she would let him have his way. Because this caused a problem during his teenage years, I encouraged her to tell Raymond "no" if I told him "no." I also explained to her, in a loving manner, that when she goes against the rules I established for Raymond, she was disrespecting my household, and more importantly, she was making it harder for him to respect my authority.

Momma said she didn't quite understand the way I did things, and that she never saw a household managed like mine. I knew she was concerned about us, but I don't think she really comprehended the depth of my struggle. It wasn't possible for her to understand the way I did things. I was a single woman raising a male child, so how could she?

Momma also thought I was too strict on Raymond sometimes. But of course, it was because she was only listening to his side of the story. Once I gave her my explanation, she understood why I had to be tough on him.

I'm sure Raymond locking me out of the house one day helped her to realize that I had to be hard on him to keep him under control. I had punished him by taking away his car, and he came up with the bright idea to lock me out of the house. It took momma to talk to him and persuade him to finally open the door. (*Okay, I know you're wondering why he's still breathing*).

◇·◇·◇·◇

When Raymond turned twenty, momma was still giving him what she called "extra spending change." When I asked her why she was still giving him money, she explained that she wanted to help me out because I was a single parent. I informed her that Raymond was now a young man and responsible for his own needs. But I could tell, to her, he was still her curly headed grandson, who often played in the dirt in her backyard.

I imagine momma was afraid that when Raymond grew up, their closeness would end. So to comfort her, whenever he went to visit, I decided not to ask her if she gave him any extra money to spend. I wanted to allow her to be the "grandmother next door" the best way she knew how.

On one hand, momma living next door was sometimes a challenge, especially when Raymond was upset with me and would run to her because I didn't let him have his way. Fortunately, momma and I learned to work together to make sure he didn't use the two of us against each other.

On the other hand, having momma close by was the best blessing a single parent could have. Momma not only provided an abundance of wisdom and support, she also made the best fried chicken, mustard greens, sweet potatoes, and peach cobbler on this side of heaven!

Life Lesson #14

Families can help support each other in a plethora of ways. When others show acts of kindness that create a challenge between the parent and the child, these areas of conflict should be addressed immediately.

Most often, those giving a helping hand don't always realize they are creating a conflict. These issues should be handled gently, with the child's best interest in mind.

Chapter 15

✍

LOVE IS NOT ENOUGH
More Tough Love Is

ALTHOUGH RAYMOND WAS still living at home, he was definitely at the age where he should have understood that being an adult meant being responsible. We had many talks about how our choices determine our future, but for some reason he wasn't taking life seriously.

I had just returned from vacation, and Mr. Robinson, who was recommended by a good friend to do house repairs, was replacing the rotten wood on the exterior of my house. He asked me if I could go to the hardware store and pick up some additional supplies before I went to work.

Raymond was still asleep, so I woke him up and asked him to go with me to the hardware store. When I was ready to leave, I called for him, but he was still in bed.

"Raymond, I need you to go with me and bring the supplies back to Mr. Robinson!" I said anxiously.

"I'm not ready to get up!" he responded.

"I don't care if you're not ready to get up! You're supposed to be out looking for a job anyway!" But Raymond *still* didn't budge.

"This can't be happening," I said, while pacing the floor. "Now, I know I am going to be late for work."

"This boy is about to push me over the edge! For the life of me, I don't know why he's trippin'! We've been over the house rules a million times, and he has the audacity to *still* be in bed!"

House Rules: If you don't have a job, you have to get up and leave the house when I go to work. While I'm at work, you cannot be in the house enjoying the benefits of my hard earned money, watching television, and eating the food I bought. When you are not working, your JOB is to FIND A JOB!

My friend, Meechie, had previously asked me why I had so many rules. I'm sure she had noticed that the rules I established for Raymond, really held *me* in bondage. Although I realized she meant I needed to have a balance, my house rule about Raymond finding a job was one rule I strictly enforced.

"Raymond, I'm going to count to thirty. If you don't get up, I'm going to really be mad," I said quietly, but angrily, all the while trying to maintain my cool, so Mr. Robinson, who was outside, couldn't hear the commotion.

"What is wrong with this boy?" I whispered under my breath. I stood in Raymond's doorway and counted slowly, trying to give him one more chance. "One, two, three, four, five...," I paused to see if he had moved, and then, I continued, "six, seven, eight...," and before I could say nine, with his head under the covers, he abruptly blurted out, "Thirty! Just say thirty, momma!"

"Raymond, if you don't get up *now*, I'm going to call the police!" I shouted. But Raymond still didn't get up. And, without hesitation, I picked up the phone and dialed 9-1-1.

By the time the police arrived, Raymond had already gone next door to my mother's house, so I spoke with the police and told them what happened. A few minutes later, Raymond casually walked out of the house, got in his car, and drove away.

After the police left, I went next door and apologized to momma for Raymond bringing her into this mess. She was extremely upset, mainly because the neighbors were watching.

"The police aren't always going to be so kind to Raymond you know! They could mistake one harmless move he makes for a threat, and your son would be dead!" momma explained.

Although I was embarrassed, I assured her it wouldn't happen again. "This will be the last time I rely on the police to stand in the gap for the lack of male authority in his life," I told myself. At that moment, I realized if Raymond's behavior was causing me to react this way, it was time for him to move out on his own.

Evidently, Mr. Robinson had been watching the whole thing from the backyard. Still in awe, it seemed as though I had just appeared in a drama scene from a movie. Somewhere between momma's house and my backyard, like Clark Kent changing into superman, I shifted my mindset and acted as though it had been a normal morning.

As I proceeded to tell Mr. Robinson that I was on my way to the hardware store, he informed me that he was proud of the way I handled the situation with Raymond. "Ms. Benita, most mothers would not have done that. I know it was hard for you, but it was really for your son's *own* good!"

~·~·~·~

Because I wanted the process for Raymond to move out to be quick, I decided to help him find an apartment. I knew if I completely left it up to him, it would take another six months, and I couldn't allow *that* to happen.

One day, on my way home from the cleaners, the "Ninety-nine Dollar Move-In Special" sign at the Riverfront apartments caught my eye. I didn't need to take a tour to determine if Raymond would like the apartments. The move-in special was enough to satisfy me, and frankly, that was all that mattered.

Raymond had some money saved, so he was able to pay his first months rent without my assistance. I was overjoyed that he was finally going to experience life on his own as an adult.

The first time his electricity was cut off, I chuckled. This was one life lesson I had been waiting for him to experience. With eagerness for him to learn how to survive on his own, I quickly assured him, "Raymond, you will be fine. When you get paid, go to the electric company and pay your bill. It won't take them long to turn your lights back on."

After being on his own for one year, apparently Raymond's eyes were open to the importance of having a college degree. When his apartment lease ended, he decided to go away to college, so he didn't renew his lease.

"Raymond, you can't just quit your good job and go away to school! You can go to school part-time and still keep your job!" I stated in a panic.

But with conviction, Raymond stated his plans. Without my knowledge, he had applied to several colleges, and had received a track scholarship. I slightly smiled to myself knowing this was the initiative I had been waiting to see in him for a long time, but why *now*? I wondered. This did not fit my plans at all.

I was excited that Raymond wanted to go to college, but I wanted him to be totally self-sufficient. After all, I spent the last twenty-three years sacrificing for him, sending him to private schools, and giving him the best of everything. It was my time now! (*Wow! What a prideful attitude*).

In my heart, I really knew it was God who had supplied our needs. Without realizing it, my heart had become bitter. I was secretly discontent because Raymond didn't go to college right after he graduated from high school. I carried my bitterness around like the Hunchback of Notre Dame carried his hump, and I'm sure Raymond felt it in every word I spoke.

I prayed,
"Dear Lord, please forgive my pride. Please, help me to keep my heart pure before You."

✍✍✍

Two weeks before school started, I decided to rent a car and take Raymond to enroll in school. This was the least I could do to support his decision, and prove to myself that I was no longer holding on to any bitterness, and all was forgiven.

As circumstances would have it, Raymond was sick the day he was supposed to move out of his apartment. When he asked me to help him clean up, I was outraged.

"Where are all your buddies that crashed at your place over the last year?" I asked unsympathetically.

"There is no way I'm going to help you clean this place! I've worked hard all week, and I want to relax and enjoy my weekend!" I said selfishly, paying no attention to the fact that he was sick. But as time quickly began to pass, I realized Raymond had made a positive choice to go to college. But, despite my ranting and raving, with compassion, I pitched in to help clean his apartment.

✍✍✍

While driving Raymond to college a few weeks later, he sadly expressed, "Momma, don't' get me wrong, you did a great job raising me, but if I had been raised with a father in the home, things would be different. Fathers just see things from a different perspective."

Although Raymond had made an important decision to further his education and move forward in life, he didn't quite know how to explain what he was feeling, but his facial expression showed it all. The pain in his soul from missing his father was still very much alive.

Life Lesson #15

Parenting is not an easy task. We unselfishly give of ourselves and often do without the things we desire, to provide for the needs of our children. Our ability to sacrifice for them is driven by our unconditional love and desire for their well-being. Although the sacrifice is challenging and demanding, the end results are rewarding.

When we always give our best, through the ups of downs of parenting, our joy will be sustained. As a parent, I didn't always make the right choices, but I was determined to love my son unconditionally, no matter what challenges we faced.

Chapter 16

✧

OIL CHANGES
Preventive Maintenance

A S NEAL PLACED the big piece of card board underneath my car, he eagerly stated, "Benita, I want you to see this!" It was freezing cold outside, and the last thing I wanted to do was get underneath my car! But Neal wanted *me* to see what was causing the oil to leak, so I would be aware of what to look for if it ever happened again. To prevent bigger problems from occurring, he never failed to emphasize the importance of taking immediate action if the car wasn't running properly.

Although Neal and my mother were no longer married, he continued to be a part of my life. Every three months he would not only check the oil in my car, he made sure everything under the hood was in tip-top shape. I could have taken my car to the dealer, but I was always confident that when Neal worked on my car, it was ready for the road.

Whenever Neal gave me advice about my car, I took it to heart. Sometimes I was so focused on the household chores, that I missed some of the details. When I would ask him to repeat something again, he would always say, "You may want to write this down." (*With all the advice he had given me over the years, I should be able to take a car apart and put it back together*).

Neal not only worked on my car, he also did small repairs around my house. Sometimes while working on one thing, if he saw something else that needed to be repaired, he magnanimously fixed it without me asking.

Neal seemed to have a strange way of determining the amount he charged me to do the repairs. Instead of ten dollars, he would charge seven dollars, or instead of twenty-five dollars, he would charge twenty-two dollars. He must have known being a single parent was quite a financial struggle for me. Without a doubt, he saw my struggle. Although I never figured out his method, I imagined he saw me as one of his daughters, and calculated the charge based on a father's love.

❧❧❧

The single parent usually has the sole responsibility of maintaining the household. Already juggling too many balls, the demands of life require "super-mom" or "super-dad" to keep adding more. The balls in the air are falling, and the parent, being busy trying to keep it all together, unfortunately neglects to see what issues are developing internally in their child.

Even in two parent homes, the demands of parenting can be overwhelming. Family time is often replaced with dad taking his son to football practice, and mom taking her daughter to ballet, and ain't nobody talking. It's only after their children have made mistakes that are "hush-hush" and hidden in the closet with the rest of the "family secrets," that the parents begin to wonder how they missed the signs.

Because parenting can be challenging, sometimes parents turn a deaf ear to addressing the "root" causes of their children's issues. When the "root" causes are not dealt with, parents often respond precipitously with discipline; and more importantly, the crux of the problem doesn't get resolved.

≈·≈·≈

Neal knew bigger problems would occur if I didn't get regular oil changes, or take immediate action to fix the problem that was causing my car not to run properly. Our children are more important and more valuable than a car or anything material for that matter, yet it seems our first inclination is to care for our material things and neglect addressing our children's issues.

At times, I was distracted by other demands and missed some of the details Neal had explained about my car, and eventually, I had to pay for costly repairs. Unfortunately, these same demands kept me from being alert to some of the issues Raymond had developed. Because these issues weren't addressed, the consequences we both suffered were great.

It is imperative to take a serious look at the factors that cause our children to misbehave. Whether the child's disruptive behavior stems from an absentee parent or not progressing in school—the first step is to admit something is broken. It is incomprehensible to think that the effects of childhood issues will disappear just because they are not addressed. The truth of the matter is that unresolved childhood issues have damaging, long-lasting effects which are most often perpetuated from generation to generation.

Life Lesson #16

Many problems in adulthood stem from unresolved childhood issues. As cars need regular maintenance for optimal performance, to prepare children to become healthy, responsible adults, parents must roll up their sleeves and take an active roll in continuously making sure their children's issues are resolved effectively.

Chapter 17

✍

HELLO, MR. ROBINSON
Cobwebs, Water Leaks, and Diamond Rings

SHOPPING ON THE *Plaza* in Kansas City with Sarah, my high school friend, was one of my favorite weekend get-a-ways. Sarah wasn't married, nor had any children of her own, so this led me to believe was the reason for her always considerably calm demeanor. Although we didn't talk much throughout the year, once we were together our constant chatter and laughter filled every waking moment like the downpour of spring rain.

We pranced through the streets of the *Plaza* like young high school girls without a care in the world. We went from store to store looking through the windows, until sparkling diamonds, attractively displayed, caught our eyes. "Diamonds!" they say, "are a girl's best friend!"

While I looked at the elegantly designed rings, Sarah was across the store looking at diamond earrings. I had always wanted to buy myself a special piece of jewelry after Raymond graduated from high school, but could never find the perfect ring for the perfect price.

Surprisingly, I spotted the same ring I had seen back home, but couldn't bring myself to buy. It had two small diamonds on each side and a blue sapphire stone in the center.

When I placed the ring on my finger, it was the perfect fit. I knew for sure this was the ring I really wanted. "I definitely can't let this opportunity pass me by again," I thought to myself.

"Oh, Sarah!" I cried out. "This is so beautiful!"

"Well, why don't you buy it, then?" Sarah responded.

Sarah didn't understand that it wasn't that simple for me. Immediately, like breaking news flashing at the bottom of the television screen, my budget flashed across my mind with one hundred and one reasons why I shouldn't buy the ring.

As the guilt of just thinking about buying the ring began to taunt me, my emotions began to boil over inside. To relax myself, I walked over to Sarah as she was holding the diamond earrings up to her ears.

"I like these two. These are the earrings I want," she told the sales clerk.

"She's paying two hundred dollars for earrings! How can she be so calm and so assured with no second thoughts?" I whispered under my breath.

Sarah gave the clerk her credit card, and then, looked at me and asked, "So, what are you going to do?"

My heart was pounding fast! "I don't know! I just don't know if I should buy this ring!"

"You can always bring it back within thirty days if you take it home and later decide you don't want it," the clerk explained.

"Perfect, that was just the escape clause I was looking for," I said to myself. I paid for my new ring and walked out of the store. I safely tucked my receipt in a safe place in my wallet, just in case my emotions overturned my decision to for once, buy something *just* for me.

As we continued to shop for sales, Sarah spotted one of her favorite stores. When we walked in, the clearance signs caught our attention and the race for bargain shopping began.

Sarah loved bright colors; she would prefer to be buried alive before wearing anything black or brown. Different shades of yellow and pink were the colors Sarah's world was made of. I longed to be part of Sarah's rainbow filled world, but could never figure out how to get there.

We walked around the store for a few minutes until Sarah spotted a sales rack filled with an array of colorful tops. As she began searching through the clothes rack, she saw the peculiar look on my face.

"Just because I like it doesn't mean you have to like it," she stated matter-of-factly, while holding a multi-colored top up against her.

"She just doesn't get it," I thought to myself. "I'm desperately trying to break out of the box of wearing every shade of black, gray, and brown known to man." To me, these colors represented the fuddy-dud mom I had become. I longed to wear the daffodil yellows and rose petal pinks, but like a magnet, I seemed to always be drawn to the "darker than night," blasé colors.

I picked out several different outfits and went into the dressing room to try them on. Piece after piece, I looked at the price tag and tried to figure out where I could cut back in my budget to buy a new outfit. "Maybe I won't buy groceries next week, or I can put only fifteen dollars in the gas tank instead of twenty-five dollars," I calculated in my mind.

Sarah had already picked out what she wanted and was waiting for me to decide. I could plainly see that her once calm demeanor had turned into frustration.

"Oh, no! Not again!" was the expression written all over Sarah's face.

"Girl, which outfits do you like?"

"Oh, Sarah!" I exclaimed pitifully, "I don't know which outfit I like best! Please ask the sales lady to bring me another size!"

As I sat in the dressing room, I became disgusted with myself. My heart began to pound like the drums in a movie scene of explorers being chased by wild animals.

"God, please tell me why I am like this? Why can't I just choose an outfit and buy it without my heart beating rapidly?"

Sarah brought me another size, which I really hadn't planned on trying on. I had only sent her out of the dressing room so I could make a decision, before she thought I was *truly* out of my mind.

In desperation, I looked through the pile of clothes I had already carried into the dressing room, and at the clothes Sarah had brought to me, as though a pair of pants or top was going to magically say, "Pick me! Pick me!" But since that was not going to happen, I finally rationalized buying two pair of khakis based on the fact that I needed them for work.

"Girl, I'm never shopping with you again!" Sarah said in frustration, as we left the store.

I walked out of the store feeling ashamed, wondering if Sarah was really serious. What started out to be an exciting shopping adventure had turned into a shopping day from hell!

◦◦◦

After I returned home from Kansas City, Mr. Robinson began working on the interior of my house. When he repaired the exterior, to keep the expenses down I helped him with the repairs as much as I could. Prayerfully, I hoped that he would allow me to assist with the interior repairs as well.

Mr. Robinson first installed extra electrical sockets in almost every room. After he hung up new window blinds, he began to remodel the bathroom. By this time, we had established a friendly, respectful rapport. He told me about his daughters, and I talked to him about my son and the challenges of being a single parent.

When Mr. Robinson removed the bathroom sink, he jokingly stated that it looked like a prison sink because it was so small. I laughed hysterically because I knew he was right.

He completely tore out the bathroom floor because of a water leak, and replaced the wood. Over the years, I had delayed repairing the water leak because it wasn't in my budget, and it didn't seem to be causing a real problem. Unfortunately, I didn't see the real effects of the overall damage underneath the linoleum, until the floor started sinking. "Never let a water leak go for a long time," Mr. Robinson calmly pointed out. "It always creates a bigger problem if it's not fixed immediately."

Each day, I rushed home enthusiastically on my lunch hour to see what he had accomplished. After he pulled the tiles off the walls that were around the bathtub, I was able to see the rusted nails, along with the dirt and cobwebs that had settled there over the years. Before now, I had never imagined what was living inside the walls of my bathroom.

Mr. Robinson hired a crew to put in the new tiles around the bathtub and on the bathroom floor. As I watched their progress, I grew excited that my tiny dollhouse bathroom was turning into a new luxurious room where I could relax.

The next morning Mr. Robinson sent me to the hardware store to buy a soap dish for the bathtub.

"Oh, that will be easy!" I expressed with much excitement. "I will be right back!" And as usual, I drove quickly to the store, so I wouldn't be late for work.

As I walked down the isle looking for a soap dish, my excitement quickly turned to disappointment. There wasn't a big selection, so naturally, I bought the cheapest one.

When I returned home and gave Mr. Robinson the soap dish, he looked at it, and then, looked at me in amazement.

"Are you sure this is the soap dish you want?" he asked.

"I guess," I responded without giving it much thought.

Mr. Robinson must have known that I didn't put forth any effort in picking out the soap dish. I'm sure he could tell it was the least expensive one on the shelf.

All of a sudden, he blurted out, "You need to start buying what you like! Those days of you buying *only* what you need, are over! Just like you decided to buy a new car, you need to buy the things *you* like!"

When Mr. Robinson first started fixing the repairs on my home, I had been driving my Pontiac Sunbird for ten years. A few weeks after he began working, I bought a new car because I needed dependable transportation to drive an hour away for piano lessons.

I told Mr. Robinson I would exchange the soap dish during my lunch break. He had spoken to me with such authority, that it penetrated my soul, and I cried like a baby all the way to work.

During the years of being a single parent, I had failed to buy the things I liked and only bought the things I needed. Apparently, this affected the filtering system within my decision making process. This unhealthy thought pattern was naturally activated every time I would buy something other than of necessity.

A few days later, Mr. Robinson and I went shopping for new bathroom accessories. As he pushed the cart, I walked down the isles like a little girl picking out furniture for her doll house. I finally chose a beautifully designed cherry wood cabinet with a marble sink and a medicine cabinet to match. He put these items on the cart, and off we went to search for a water faucet.

After I questioned Mr. Robinson about the quality of the different brands of faucets, I finally chose a beautifully designed faucet with ivory handles. Lastly, I picked out a light fixture to go over the bathroom sink and headed to the cash registers at the front of the store to pay for my items.

The sales lady rang up the items. "One thousand, twenty-five dollars and sixty cents," she stated.

Surprisingly, Mr. Robinson and I looked at each other at the same time.

"I wondered if you knew how much all this was going to cost before you got to the register," Mr. Robinson said with a smile on his face.

"I had *some* idea. But it's okay, because this time, I picked out all the things that *I* like," I responded calmly, as I laughed within myself. Mr. Robinson didn't have any idea that I had been set free from the unhealthy mindset that often caused me to panic whenever I bought things other than of necessity. The powerful words he had spoken to me the day I bought the soap dish, had freed from the bondage that had me enslaved for so many years.

Life Lesson #17

The struggles of parenting can have damaging affects on our souls. Without realizing it, parents can become locked in unhealthy thought patterns.

Our actions are a true reflection of the activity within our souls. By piercing through to the deepest part of our being, we can unravel the chords that have entangled us, and free ourselves from their relentless grip.

A Father's Voice

A father's voice
Shapes the destiny of his children.
His instructions build a solid foundation.

A father's voice
Is the voice of authority longing to be heard
When children need direction.

A father's voice
Represents a pillar of strength and protection.
His unconditional love will sustain his children for a lifetime!

Chapter 18

✌

DADDY'S BABY GIRL
A Father's Voice

ALTHOUGH IT HAD been over four months since our church changed the service time to ten o'clock, my body was still in sync with the eleven o'clock service. Each Sunday, like a fire truck racing to put out a fire, I would frantically speed down the highway and arrive in time to hear the last praise and worship song. Sunday just didn't seem like Sunday, until I had a chance to hear the praise team sing in a harmony that resounded like a host of angels.

Even though it was October, it was an unbelievably warm afternoon this particular Sunday. It was a perfect day for a picnic or a stroll in the park, but Sunday after church was the time I set aside to visit my father. Because he lived thirty minutes away, I knew if I didn't go see him as planned, I wouldn't be able to visit him until the following weekend.

On my way to visit my father, I stopped at Braum's and ordered the kid's meal that included a banana shake. When the server handed me a child's size shake, I almost lost my cool because it was so small. I didn't want to spoil the moment, so instead I rolled down the window to feel the breeze, turned on some jazz music, and sipped slowly on my banana shake as I drove blissfully down the highway.

I reminded myself that I was trying to eat healthy, and the smaller size was better for me, anyway. Besides, it was those banana shakes, along with those homemade cinnamon rolls that I couldn't stop eating last year that sent my cholesterol level through the roof. I'm sure those tasty treats were the reason I was rushed to the emergency room and had to stay in the hospital for one night.

At my last medical exam, Dr. Woo had advised me to take a cholesterol test. I was happy to inform her that my cholesterol level should be healthy, because after my terrifying hospital visit I changed my eating habits, and started keeping track of everything I ate. She also asked me to check with my father to see if he has high cholesterol. "If you're eating healthy and exercising, it's possible your high cholesterol level could be hereditary," she informed me.

As I continued to drive leisurely down the highway, I wondered what daddy was going to say this time that would propel me into my destiny. After I arrived, I walked slowly towards the door of the nursing home to make sure I didn't disturb the big dog sleeping at the end of the long porch.

I hesitantly pushed the button that automatically unlocked the front door to the lobby. Daddy was sitting in his favorite spot. I stared at him as I walked towards him at a snail's pace, hoping he would react. But after I realized he didn't recognize me, I started our ritual of questions and answers, hoping to trigger something in his mind that would remind him that I was his baby girl.

"Hey, how ya doing?" I asked, somewhat cautiously.

"Oh, fine," he answered with a smile.

"When did you get here?"

"I just got here a few minutes ago."

"Now, how far away do you live?"

"Oh, about thirty minutes or so," I responded softly, being very careful to make sure he stayed calm.

I pushed daddy's wheelchair towards the couch, so I could sit and listen to him talk about whatever came across his mind.

"Whatcha been up to?" I asked.

"I ain't been up to nothing," he casually responded.

Daddy finally began to talk about things I definitely didn't understand, or could make sense of. Every so often I would interject and ask, "Is that right?" or "Why did they do that?" Although I couldn't tell what he was talking about, I could tell when he was passionate about something. His voice would raise a few pitches, his mouth would curve to the side, and his eyes would lighten up like a hundred watt light bulb.

After awhile, I asked daddy if he wanted to go outside to get some sunshine, but he didn't seem to understand my question. I pushed his wheelchair outside and parked it in the small strip of shade that was provided by the pole. Although it wasn't really cold outside, the slightest wind seemed to really get his attention. Whenever he felt the breeze on his face, he would close his eyes as though he was making a wish.

"Did you feel that?" daddy asked.

"Yes, daddy. Are you cold?"

"Yes," he answered softly.

"We can go back inside if you want to."

"No, I'm fine."

I laughed to myself because I realized that I inherited my nature of not liking cold weather, from daddy.

Daddy had my undivided attention. He had no idea the purpose of my visit was not only for me to spend some time with him, but for him to spend some time with me, too.

I was content listening to daddy talk about anything and everything. All the while, hoping he would tell me something to help me make sense of this thing called *life*. It didn't have to be a complete sentence, bits and pieces of the puzzle would do, and I could put them all together.

Daddy asked me if I was still doing that "outfit." I knew he meant playing the piano. On my last visit I played some classical music for him. I told him I was going to learn some church songs to play for him, too.

"I thought those were church songs!" he stated somewhat enthusiastically.

"Daddy, those were classical songs."

"They sounded like church songs to me," he stated, as he laughed slightly.

"Have you started playing anywhere yet?"

"No, I am still learning to play. I don't play that well, so I only play at home."

"You can't wait until *you* think you're good enough before you play in front of others!" he stated with conviction.

Every so often, daddy would talk about his old house. He seemed to be concerned if the grass was being cut.

"Daddy, you shouldn't worry about that. You just have to trust God."

"You can't *just* trust God!" daddy stated with passion and enthusiasm. "You *still* gotta do something!"

As I took daddy back inside, he told me he was glad I came to visit. I told him I loved him, kissed him on the cheek, and watched him as I walked slowly to the door.

Daddy kept his eyes on me while eating a chocolate chip cookie the nurse had given him. He looked at me as though he never held me in his arms, or tucked me in the bed at night. His impassive look left me feeling somewhat poignant, for his memories seemed only to be transitory. I slowly drove away, wondering if daddy knew I was his baby girl.

ↄ·ↄ·ↄ·ↄ

On my way home, I thought of the many children that have never heard their father's voice. Their anticipation of a word, a hug, or a smile from a father they have never met or rarely see, often turns into pain and crippling them in ways that go unnoticed for years, even through adulthood. Some children rise above the pain, while others spend countless number of years searching for the voice that is supposed to give them security, direction, and love.

There is no statute of limitations on the pain our children feel because of the lack of quality time with their fathers. They are hurting and angry, and are expressing it through their rebellious actions. They are crying out for help, but it seems that no one is really listening!

Life Lesson #18

Some children can assertively move forward without the presence of a father in the home, while others, naturally feeling abandoned and rejected, become locked in their pain and stagnated in their growth.

Like the Amaryllis Belladonna lily that pops up out of nowhere during the end of the summer season and before long disappears, mothers must be careful not to nonchalantly accept this similar patter from their children's fathers.

Obviously, there are some instances in which the father being in the child's life is detrimental to the child's welfare. But when this is not the case, mothers can educate the child's father of the significant impact they have on contributing to the child's success and well-being.

The Wind

Today, I let the wind blow through my hair,
To free me to walk this journey without a care.
I realized I had been holding on too tight;
Therefore, causing the struggle within me, the fight.

So I simply, let go.

Chapter 19

✍

BENITA LOUISE
Exposed

MY ANNUAL MEDICAL exam had been scheduled for over three months. I had planned to tell Dr. Woo about some of my personal issues after my exam, but when she spoke, it was as though she was beckoning me to spill my guts about my life. Without hesitation, I poured out my life to her like a water faucet turned on full power.

"My emotions seem to be out of whack, more intense than usual. My son moved back home six months ago, and my father passed away last month from complications with Alzheimer's disease. My friends seem to think that I'm going through menopause, but other than that, I have a really great life."

"I love to travel, I am learning to play the piano, and I play tennis and exercise regularly. I also tutor the kindergarten and first grade class at two different elementary schools. I am an avid reader, I write poetry and I am writing a book. But most of all, I have great friends and I love God!" I expressed passionately, trying to convince myself that I was really okay.

"What makes you think your emotions are off balance? Have you had any major traumas?" she asked.

"Oh, I've had many. From stressful childhood experiences

to two divorces, just to name a few. Oh, yeah, and single parenting has definitely been a struggle for me, too."

"What are you experiencing?" She asked.

"Well, Raymond keeps his clothes in the washroom, and he keeps it a mess. Mr. Robinson (*Remember him?*) was putting up a new door in my kitchen. He needed something to cover up the desk, so he used a sheet that was in the washroom. I was devastated knowing he saw the washroom like that, and immediately I went all out to get it totally organized. The next day, Neal came over to work on Raymond's car and he needed something out of Raymond's trunk. I opened up the trunk and it looked like a pig sty. I then said to myself, 'Oh, no! My son has a problem, and I can't fix it!'"

"Benita, you worry too much," said Dr. Woo. "You may have PTSD, Post Traumatic Stress Disorder. It seems your brain never winds down, so you are always in survival mode. This can be fixed but you must live a balanced and healthy life style. I would like you to see a counselor as soon as possible. If you are having problems sleeping, this could be one of the reasons that your cholesterol level is high."

"I also don't feel my son is where he should be at this stage of his life," I added hesitantly.

"Benita, there are *no* shoulds or shouldn'ts. Every situation in life happens for a purpose, and that purpose is — to learn! If we don't have challenges, we won't learn and we won't progress! Once you accept this as a part of life, you will be able to deal with things better! You must believe you have given your son the tools he needs, and let go! Let go of him! This is his journey! He has to find his own path and you can't script it for him! Make an appointment to see a counselor and come back and see me in three months!"

After I left the doctor's office, I immediately called my

friend, Connie. "Girl, you won't believe this. My doctor said I need to go to counseling. Clearly, she feels I need to work on some things, and hopefully Raymond will go, too. I know he's got some issues, but he won't talk about them."

"Benita, is it possible you could be going through menopause?" Connie asked. "I remember after Raymond ate your leftovers one time, you wanted to say to him, 'I'm not your prostitute, so don't be eating my food.' That would have been a bit much to express to him," she stated, as we laughed hysterically.

"Connie, can it be that I was so focused on making sure Raymond had the tools he needed, that I failed to get the tools for myself? I'm glad I don't have to go through the weekend without getting this resolved. Can you believe the counselor has an opening tomorrow? You know only God could have orchestrated that! I'll talk to the counselor and see what he thinks, and I'll get back with you tomorrow."

After I hung up the phone, without delay, I called Paula and explained to her what the doctor had said. Paula jumped right in with her diagnosis. "Louise, you must accept where you are in life as the place you are supposed to be. It's where Raymond is supposed to be. It's fine that he is at home with you for this season in his life. We rush our kids too much. We rush them to walk, we rush them to stop sucking the bottle, and we rush them to learn how to ride a bike. Once our children become adults, they will still need us in some capacity. If God didn't want us to still be their parents once they are grown, we would all die. You're putting too much pressure on yourself. You've got too many things going on, and you don't just *have* to be this great pianist!"

Although what Paula spoke made sense, it was hard for me to accept her advice. I was the one always helping others, giving advice, and being the rescuer. Now, I needed to be rescued!

ᔐᔐᔐ

Later that evening, while Raymond ironed his clothes, I relaxed on the couch and waited patiently for the opportune moment to tell him about my day.

"Well, you won't believe what happened to me today?" I said hesitantly, while trying to feel him out.

"Oh, no! What happened momma?" he asked, as though he was frightened.

"I went to the doctor."

"Did you have a pap smear?"

"No, son!" I answered shockingly, wondering how he felt so comfortable to talk to me about that kind of thing.

"She said I may have Post Traumatic Stress Disorder."

Raymond immediately stopped ironing and came over and sat on the table near the couch.

"I knew something was wrong with you momma," he spoke, with a genuine compassion that I hadn't felt in years.

"Remember, my major is psychology. I know a great deal about these things."

"Well, she said my emotions were intense due to unresolved issues because of traumas I experienced in the past, so I'm going to see a counselor tomorrow. Son, I'm afraid because of my unhealthy emotional responses, you may also have some unresolved issues."

"Momma, I'm fine. I dealt with my issues at church during the Men's Gathering. Maybe you should go to the one they have for women. You know, there, they help you dig into your past to help you resolve your issues. I had never seen so many grown men cry before."

I slowly followed Raymond to his room like a baby duckling following behind its mother. I had not been the perfect mother I desired to be, and it was important to me that he was empowered to reach his goals and dreams. Because of my issues and unwise choices, I knew it was quite possible I hadn't equipped him for adulthood, and I didn't want him to repeat the mistakes I made that caused me to struggle as an adult.

As I sat on his bed, I looked at him, and again sincerely stated my concern. "Son, I just want to make sure I have given you the tools to be a healthy, responsible adult."

"Momma, you *have* given me the tools. You're right. I'm not organized and my room is not always clean, but what else am I *not* doing? I go to work, I pay my bills and I pay you rent. I am being responsible. I am taking care of myself. I haven't asked you for any money in a long time."

Raymond was right. I couldn't think of anything he was doing for me to declare him irresponsible. Everything else was really minor, like the time he drank all the orange juice and I swore I would never buy any more until he moved out.

"Perhaps Connie was right. Maybe I am going through menopause," I thought to myself.

My conversation with Raymond went way too smooth, maybe because I was the one with the problem this time, and I wasn't pouncing on him for something he had done that didn't fit into my perfect world. He was out of the spotlight, so we were able to finally talk like two adults.

"Raymond, all I want is to know that I am loved and appreciated, and I will give you the same respect."

"Momma, I can do that!" he eagerly agreed.

✌∙✌∙✌∙✌

The past two days had been unbelievably stressful for me. It seemed as though I was reliving the pain I experienced when I watched my father die in the nursing home. I felt that someone was holding my head under water, and as I would fight to come up for air, in between every breath I was also trying to save him.

The doctor had previously written me a prescription for sleeping pills, but Paula had begged me not to take them. "Louise, there are other ways to relax. Meditate or listen to soft music, just find a healthier way to fall asleep. Those sleeping pills cause a lot of health problems and are very addictive!"

I knew I definitely needed something to help me relax, so I decided to rent a movie. A dose of a good comedy was sure to make me laugh and help me fall asleep. I also decided to buy the pills anyway, just in case the movie didn't do the trick.

The information sheet attached to the sleeping pills contained a long list of side effects that ranged from nausea, difficulty in breathing, and nervousness; to disorientation, dizziness and seizures. "I'd rather not be able to sleep than suffer from these side effects," I muffled under my breath. Down the toilet they went. "I'm going to make sure nobody gets their hands on these things."

As I began to watch the movie, I noticed one of the characters was high strung, always on guard, and definitely determined to win. But after thirty minutes into the movie, I was so relaxed, I drifted off to asleep.

The next morning as I finished watching the movie, I realized I had a lot of similarities as the character who was overly emotional. And I laughed within myself because I had just seen a display of my behavior when I am under stress.

"No wonder my emotions are so whacky! I'm *just* like her!" I said to myself in total amazement.

Watching the movie had given me a clearer picture of what was going on with me. Because I had slept peaceably through the night without taking any medication, I knew it would only be a matter of time until I would be able to turn the page to this chapter in my life. I was soon to become a new and improved *"Benita Louise!"*

~~~

As I sat in the counselor's office preparing to reveal my most private inner thoughts, I wondered, "How the heck did I get here? This was definitely not on my agenda at the beginning of the week."

I was about to internally strip down, like taking a yearly physical at the doctor's office. This was something I had never done before, at least not to this degree. The *real* Benita was about to be exposed, and my mind was racing with a million thoughts and a million questions. What should I expect? Should I tell him everything?

After looking back over my life, I realized I was like a time bomb ready to explode at any sign of stress. "For over twenty years, I've hidden my pain, and tried to keep up the image that I had it all together...*But No More!*" I declared.

"For once and for all, this is it!" I said persuasively, trying to encourage myself. "Whatever I need to say or do to be free, I must do it. This will be the first time I've really exposed myself to the truth about what's going on with me!"

∽∾∽∾

As the counselor came in, I was rehearsing in my mind what I would say to him when he inquired about the purpose of my visit. I didn't want him to think I was really *that* bad off. I'm sure he had seen my kind before—not wanting to admit the real truth, that they really had a problem.

"Benita, what's going on?" the counselor asked, as he sat in the chair directly across from me.

"Well, my emotions seem to be out of whack lately. My friends say I'm going through menopause and that I am putting too much pressure on myself," I responded eloquently, trying to be calmer than my outburst in the doctor's office the day before, hoping just maybe, he would overlook the obvious.

"What kind of traumas have you experienced?"

"Oh, no! Not again!" I thought to myself.

In that moment, I closed my eyes to recapture the painful pictures that my mind had taken throughout my life, and hesitantly explained, "Over the years, being a single parent has really taken a toll on me. I've been married and divorced twice, and my father passed away last month."

"Anything else?" the counselor asked with compassion.

"As an adult, I find myself running away from confrontation. The effects of my parents' divorce when I was a child have often made it hard for me to deal with conflict head on. Besides that," I added apprehensively, "I was molested as a child."

"Oh, I see. You've really had some tough situations. Have you ever talked about any of this?"

"Not really. I believed that because I was strong I would survive, and my son and I would be fine."

I also explained to the counselor how I over reacted when I saw Raymond's room and car in a mess.

"Benita, because your belief is that Raymond's room and car is a reflection on you as a parent, it triggered your emotions intensely, and that is what caused your reaction," he explained. "It seems to me," he added, "you have an exaggerated personal control because you were molested. You were controlled against your will, probably by someone you trusted, and this is how you keep others from controlling you. Because your subconscious still remembers the trauma, many things can trigger your emotions and take you back in your mind to the exact moment of the trauma as though you are experiencing it today. Your thoughts are causing you to overreact, so you must change your perception of the trauma, and see what happened to you, the way God sees it."

"You will definitely have to do some inner work," the counselor explained. "Your beliefs cause your thoughts, your thoughts cause your feelings, and your feelings cause your actions. The negative feelings and actions should signal there is something going on with your core beliefs that you need to examine. Each trauma you experienced created a negative belief in your mind; therefore, you must replace the negative belief with a positive belief, which is the truth, from the word of God."

I also expressed to the counselor that I felt Raymond was unorganized because of his unresolved issues, and that I believed it was my responsibility to help him overcome these issues. I informed him that I was truly concerned that I didn't give him all the tools he needed to be a responsible adult. The counselor again simply stated that I need to exchange my core belief from, "Raymond's room is a reflection on me as a parent," to "Raymond is an adult and it's fine if the way he keeps his room and car does not meet my expectations."

As the counselor took a few minutes to write some notes on his pad, I reflected over the advice he had given me. His explanation of the cause of my unhealthy emotions was life changing. He also demonstrated a more practical approach in analyzing life's challenging situations. Although his solutions seemed simple, I knew I had to take the time to change my way of thinking.

"Benita, keep in mind," the counselor added, "if you feel Raymond living with you is a problem, you should discuss this with him. It may be time for him to get his own place."

On my way home from the counselor's office, I called Rhonda to catch her up on what was happening on "The Days of Our Lives." (*And I definitely wasn't talking about the daytime soap opera*). Rhonda had always been a true friend and never had a problem expressing her thoughts, especially when I did things that just didn't make sense.

"Rhonda, do you remember when you asked me, why do I keep choosing the wrong husbands?"

"Oh, Louise! Did I ask you that? That was wrong of me."

"Don't worry Rhonda. It's okay," I assured her. "I now have the answer to that question. Besides not having the tools for marriage, the love and affection I felt for the two men I chose to marry were not enough to sustain a marriage. My unresolved issues and unrealistic perceptions, mixed with their unresolved issues and unrealistic perceptions were definitely not the ingredients for a lasting and happy marriage. Over the years, I've been making decisions based on my emotions and unrealistic expectations, and I've been raising Raymond with these same misguided perceptions." I explained compellingly.

"Louise, you're trying to make Raymond fit the mold you designed for him! You want him to be more successful than you are! He has his own way of doing things, so you can't control him!" Rhonda expressed convincingly.

"Control him is the last thing I want to do! I want him to be free to be the man he chooses to become!" I explained.

After talking to Rhonda, I realized my own issues and fears were getting in the way of my son being an independent adult. Sadly, my issues were not only affecting me, but crippling Raymond as well.

Although I believed that I was a strong woman of faith, through my life experiences, fear had crept into my soul and adversely affected my thought processes. A lot of my decisions had been based on my own underlying fears of making mistakes and struggling financially. Because of these fears, unconsciously, I tried to prevent negative things from happening to Raymond by trying to control him.

∽∽∽

Every since Raymond moved back home, I found myself

trying to raise an adult. To make sure he was doing things "the right way," hence, "my way," I tried to correct any little thing I saw him do that didn't meet my expectations.

Because Raymond was still living with me, I failed to see that he was already a man. So in a panic, I went back into survival mode. Without realizing it, I was trying to give him the tools he already had. Rather than seeing the situation as Raymond repositioning himself for success, I took it upon myself to be responsible for him again. I tried to prevent him from making mistakes, instead of seeing the mistakes as learning tools. Consequently, my method of parenting had an adverse effect on both of us, and had made parenting for me a constant struggle.

◈◈◈

I began the journey of raising Raymond by praying for God to teach him how to be a man. I initially failed to see that God was doing this by allowing both of us to go through tough times and giving us strategies along the way to overcome them.

Raymond walked with me through my struggles, perhaps locking up his own emotions and expressing his pain in ways I didn't understand. Although he couldn't comprehend the depth of my pain, he always seemed to know when I was hurting and would express his love for me the best way a son could for his mother.

I believe God gave Raymond to me to help me break free from my issues, and the grip of fear that often kept me from pursuing my goals and dreams. I had been afraid to fall, afraid that I might lose everything I had worked hard for. As I struggled to give Raymond the tools to be a responsible adult, God used him to help me acquire the tools I needed for my journey.

Life Lesson #19

More than likely, we have all experienced some degree of trauma in our lives and are affected by PTSD, (Post Traumatic Stress Syndrome). Because there are varying levels of trauma, there are also various ways of expressing the pain of the trauma; therefore, the way we interpret these life events, determines their effects on our lives.

Our perception of the trauma can cause damaging effects to our core being. When we only medicate the symptoms and not effectively deal with the issues caused by the trauma, our lives will continually display the afflictions within our souls.

Even though our thoughts may cause us to react negatively, we are *not* our thoughts. The word of God emphatically tells us that we are wonderfully made; therefore, we should not define ourselves by the situations that happen to us.

There's a price to pay for freedom.
In order to be free, I had to be transparent . . .
Not only to free myself, but to help free others.

And you shall know the truth,
And the truth shall make you free (John 8:32).

It's Over Now

It's over now.
It's over now.
The pain of your past is over now.

The chains have been broken.
Your soul has been set free.
Live in your purpose!
Be all that you can be!

It's over now!

Chapter 20

✍

INTRODUCING AMY
The Amygdala

A FTER I ARRIVED home from the counselor's office, I sat on my bed and analyzed what he had explained. Being adamant about changing my unhealthy responses, I made a list of all the traumas I experienced and how they impacted my life. I also wrote down the negative perceptions the traumas had created, how they affected my mindset, and the emotional reactions that would occur when I experienced stress. Then, I proceeded to write down the healthy way that I should respond to each situation, and the corresponding thought process that would allow me to react effectively.

Being excited about gaining an understanding of how the "mind" works, I immediately began to work on changing my unrealistic perceptions and replacing them with more constructive and practical ones. By doing this inner work, it moved me away from my usual thought process that caused me to overact. This allowed me to utilize a more logical method in dealing with stressful situations, which resulted in a change in my reactions.

After a few months of working on my inner self, I was eager to know if Raymond noticed the changes in my responses, so I asked him if he had seen a change in me.

"Yes, momma, I have seen a change in you," he replied.

A little tear trickled down the side of my face. I really didn't have to ask, but I wanted to hear it from him. Being able to laugh with my son on a day-to-day basis and talk about difficult situations without reacting emotionally, to me, was a definite indication that my negative perceptions had started to change. As a result, Raymond's attitude also changed.

∽∽∽

My unresolved childhood issues often caused me to hide my emotions whenever I became overwhelmed. Because I was molested as a child, unknowingly, I was determined to control every situation so I wouldn't be controlled by anyone again.

As a little girl, the day my emotions were damaged and severely scarred, I sat in the corner crying and locked the pain deep within my soul. Over the years, I became such a pro at hiding my pain that it took no thought to regress to that frightened little girl. In the blink of an eye, I would hide my pain in that safe place within my soul, locking up my emotions when I should have expressed myself, while at other times overreacting when the hard times were unbearable, often trying to run away from the pain.

I buried the pain of my first marriage to Raymond's father so deep, that I was sure the pain had no lasting effects on me. I was determined that my son and I would survive and still have a great life without his father. Because the underlying pain was never addressed, the pain turned into a fear of failure that negatively influenced my decisions.

During my second marriage, I displayed a whirlwind of emotions. After our divorce, I spent many years over-compensating with extremely high expectations in many areas of my life. Although my husband and I loved each other, we both had issues from our past that had not been resolved, and the effects of these issues overshadowed our love.

·~·~·~·

It was time for my three month checkup with Dr. Woo. She wanted to keep on top of how I was managing my stress and emotions since our last visit.

"Benita, life can be very challenging," she previously expressed to me. "Everyone has to deal with stress, but the key is learning how to manage it. Continuous periods of unmanaged stress can cause damaging effects to your body. As I've mentioned over the years, if you can't handle the stress on your job, you should find another place to work. But since you can't find a new family, you must find ways to balance your life," she stated with much concern.

When she walked in, I immediately informed her that I didn't take the sleeping pills she prescribed because the side effects were far too damaging, and that I had found healthier ways to help me fall asleep. I eagerly expressed that I had been working on changing my thought processes and had already experienced positive changes on how I reacted under stress.

"Benita, the prescription I gave you was a very small dosage. You wouldn't have been affected by the side effects," Dr. Woo explained. "Your blood pressure is still a little high, so I need to check it again."

The nurse had taken my blood pressure when I first arrived. When she told me the reading, I quickly let her know it couldn't be right. I had been eating healthy, watching my sodium intake, and exercising almost every day.

When the doctor took my blood pressure again, the reading was normal. "Benita, I believe you have the "fight or flight" syndrome. I'm going to give you a prescription to help retrain your amygdala."

"Fight or flight" syndrome! What is that?" I asked suspiciously.

"When you first came in, you were probably nervous and

stressed, and your blood pressure became elevated. After you sat down and relaxed for a while, it returned back to normal. Are you still having problems sleeping?" she asked.

"Sometimes," I responded hesitantly.

"You must learn to relax more. Do you ever have dreams?"

"No, I really don't think so."

"It's because you're not getting a deep sleep," she stated. "I'm going to prescribe some sleeping pills for you. I want you to take these so you can get a deeper sleep. Your body needs at least seven or eight hours of sleep to restore itself and fight off diseases and infections."

I left the doctor's office that day curious about that "fight or flight" thing. "Amygdala—what on earth is an amygdala?" I wondered. "When I get home, I'm going to look that word up on the internet. Why would I need medication to retrain my brain?" I asked myself.

By the time I arrived home, I was already focused on something else and didn't look up the word "amygdala." And that night, I decided to take the sleeping pills for thirty days to ensure I would get the adequate amount of sleep I needed.

After a month passed, I was sleeping like a baby and had forgotten about the "amygdala" all together. (*After I stopped taking the sleeping pills, I began to experience withdrawal symptoms. Because I had already started balancing my life, I was keenly aware of these symptoms and the effect the pills had on my body. If I had taken the pills for a longer period of time, it was highly possible; I could have become addicted to the medication*).

·*♪·♪·♪·♪*

Like clockwork, everyday at 10:00 A.M. and 3:00 P.M., I would change into my tennis shoes and run down the back stairs at work, to start my fifteen minute break. Dr. Woo previously expressed to me the importance of walking thirty minutes a day to manage stress and lower my cholesterol, so I incorporated walking as part of my daily routine.

Once I made it down the stairs and outside, my routine would begin. I would put my hair in a ponytail, tuck my ID badge and cell phone inside my jacket, and gaze up at the security camera pointing directly at me. I often laughed to myself, wondering what security thought as they saw me do this ritual everyday. I pretended I was in training and would tell myself, "You may not be training for the Olympics, but you're definitely training for a marathon, and this marathon is called *life!*"

Most people walked each day with co-workers, chatting away about what was going on in their department or in their personal lives, but I was on a quest for knowledge, so I walked alone. I also made it a point to read something inspirational or educational as I walked.

This day was no different than the others, except at 3:00 P.M. I didn't feel like walking. It was sunny outside and the temperature was just right for playing tennis. I wanted to leave work early, but I convinced myself to stay at work because I only had one day of vacation left until the end of the year.

Finally, I decided not to go outside and walk. I logged on to the company website and browsed the list of books our company provided for the employees for personal and professional development. After a few minutes, my eyes suddenly stopped at the title, *Iconoclast: A Neuroscientist Reveals How to Think Differently,* by Gregory Berns.[1]

"That's an interesting word," I thought to myself. "Iconoclast," I repeated it in my mind again, not really paying attention to the rest of the title.

Fascinated by this word, I began to scroll through the table of contents. When I read one of the subtitles, *"Taming the Amygdala Through Reappraisal and Extinction,"*[2] I became so excited that I had to tell somebody, so I called my friend, Carla, who also worked for the company. She was the only person close by that I knew would understand my enthusiasm.

"Girl, what time are you leaving work? I've got something to show you!" I said with excitement.

"I'm leaving at four o'clock," Carla calmly stated.

Carla knew about some of my challenges as a single parent. She was also familiar with my dramatic expressions, and knew the way I express my excitement was one part of me that was probably *not* going to change.

As I walked Carla to her car, I enthusiastically began to tell her what I just learned about the amygdala.

"Girl, can you believe this is the word the doctor mentioned to me? I wasn't *even* looking for it, but somehow, it found me. Maybe this was God's way of telling me I was moving too slow. I had planned to research this word over a month ago, but I didn't. I guess God decided to intervene and give me a push."

"You know how God is," Carla stated with a big smile. "He's so awesome. He knows how to orchestrate our path, that's the beauty of it all."

After I finished talking to Carla, I went back to my desk and continued to read about the characteristics of the amygdala that were listed in Gregory Bern's book:

The amygdala is a twitchy character with a long memory. Once the amygdala encodes an unpleasant association, it doesn't forget it. These memories sometimes resurface at the most inopportune times, and in the worst of circumstances, the amygdala is responsible for traumatic flashbacks.[3]

Although key brain structures like the amygdala are responsible for the fear response, it is often formative experiences during childhood and adolescence that end up rearing their heads in adult life.[4]

One of the most effective strategies for regulating the expression of fear is through a technique called *cognitive reappraisal*. This simply means reinterpreting emotional information in such a way that the emotional component is diminished.[5]

Much of the problem with acute stressors derives from perception. Because perception is a product of the brain, reappraisal works well to change perception in such a way that the fear system is not activated.[6]

Cognitive strategies are highly effective at keeping the fear system under control, and these cognitive strategies have their origin in the prefrontal cortex in the brain. So rather than people needing to avoid the situations that cause fear or circumstances that make them stress out, neuroscience is showing how the rational part of the brain can regain control over such toxic emotions like fear.[7]

I was extremely excited to learn more about the aspects of the amygdala, the term the doctor and counselor had previously explained. Gaining more knowledge about this neurological term I called "Amy," would allow me to be more aware of the situations that trigger my negative emotions.

In the twinkling of an eye, that day my life changed *forever*. I was transformed in such a profound way, that I began telling anyone and everyone who would listen, hoping they would apply this knowledge to their own lives!

·ᔑᔑᔑ

Four months had passed since Raymond compassionately stated, "Momma, I knew something was wrong with you."

Over the years, I knew something was wrong with me too, but I couldn't quite put my finger on it.

Although I didn't fully understand the intricacies of the traumas I experienced, I was overjoyed because I didn't need a pill to retrain my amygdala, which was causing me to overreact because of traumatic flashbacks. More importantly, I had gained the knowledge to make what was "wrong" with me, "right." I only needed to invest in myself and gain the knowledge of how to deal with the traumas I experienced. Once I changed my thoughts, I had the power to change my life!

Life Lesson #20

The "busyness" in our lives keeps us moving at warp speed, and steals precious time that should be spent with our families. We are too busy to see the perpetual cycle of pain in our lives, and too busy to stop and ask ourselves the most profound question that could change the course of our lives: *Why do I act the way I do?*

Unfortunately, we have short changed ourselves by allowing society to define the meaning of success and happiness. Sadly, we have invested in material things instead of investing in what is really important, our children and our families.

We are complex beings! God fashioned us this way. When we take the time to learn about the incredible aspects of the mind, and to consider the mind as a tool that holds wisdom and knowledge to help us reach our goals and dreams, we become empowered to change our lives!

The Puzzle

I cried a lot this year.
Maybe it was good for me to release the pain and
Free my soul.

God has designed my purpose so distinctly,
Only I can walk out my own destiny.
Each of life's moments is a piece of the puzzle that will eventually be
Filled in with all of my experiences and
Will only be completed when I die.

The puzzle will have many colors.
The darkest colors will be the toughest pieces to fit in.
Because of their obscurity, these pieces may seem to mean one thing,
But will fit in a place I didn't expect.

Although it has taken awhile,
I am learning to put the dark pieces in their right perspective.
I am also learning to dance between the raindrops,
Make the sound of thunder the beat of my drum and
The lightening, my spotlight.
This is what causes the puzzle to come alive.
It causes the pinks and yellows to run into the dark colors,
Creating a color that has no name, an exuberant ray of light.
This light uncovers the darkness underneath the surface of my soul that
Tries to steal from my existence.

What is this in my soul? Where did it come from?
Life has a way of challenging us
To face every activity within the soul.
I can only hear the challenge if I pay close attention.

I'm living, but yet dying by the suffocation of my own thoughts.
I must save myself or die a slow death.
My soul, filled with anguish, releases itself
From unwanted particles that interrupt the ray of light.

Sometimes I have to move the pieces around
To put them in their right places.
This often disturbs the other pieces
That had comfortably found their right place
Within the puzzle.
It takes a lifetime to get it right.
I have the last say,
Only I know when it is a perfect fit.

The puzzle is not "one size fits all."
The frame was measured to only fit me.
There is a picture of the puzzle deep within my soul.
This picture is my destiny, my purpose.

We were all created with a purpose.
Most of us don't see the picture clearly, or
We don't like the picture we see.

Some puzzles are not even close to being completed, while others are
almost finished with the meaning still unknown.

∾∾∾

Chapter 21

✍

ALIVIA
Missing Pieces

A S I LOOKED outside through the sliding glass doors, I stared at the water flowing in the creek below Sharon's apartment. Although I wanted to sit outside on the balcony and reflect over my weekend in Kansas City, the bitter, cold weather kept me from enjoying the sound of the water racing to its destiny. In a few hours, I would be headed back home excited to continue my journey and fulfill my purpose.

I had felt the same anticipation when my mother and I first began our drive to Kansas City a few days before to visit Sharon, our long time friend. I hadn't been back to my birth place in over two years. Would things be different? Would I see someone that I grew up with and hadn't seen in many years? Would something happen to change the course of my life?

✍·✍·✍

While driving to Kansas City, I cut my cinnamon roll in half to save some for later. It was dripping with creamy frosting, but before long, it vanished like the early morning dew running from the sun on a cool autumn morning.

"Sipping on a cup of hot tea, while driving down the highway, what a wonderful place to have breakfast," I thought to myself. The wide expansion of the never-ending highway was my breakfast table, and the rainbow my tablecloth. The fields and fields of grain, cows grazing in the grass, and goats running wild were my backdrop.

Within an hour and a half, we were in Joplin, Missouri. We stopped at one of my favorite places where I often escaped from the everyday pressures of life. It was a great place to buy accessories for the new home I had been planning to buy for almost ten years, or a place for a woman in her forties to have a wedding (*that being me of course*), or just a place to bring my girlfriends for lunch for a girls' day out.

I ordered my favorite, a chicken salad sandwich on sour dough bread, and momma ordered the same. As our food was being prepared, I walked around taking pictures in my head of things I wanted to buy some day.

In passing, one lady looked at us and stated: "This place is simply beautiful. I want to be buried here."

"That's interesting!" momma said in amazement. "We were just talking about having a wedding here!"

The atmosphere was filled with the joyful Christmas Spirit, and holiday decorations were attractively displayed.

"This year I'm going to go all out for Christmas," I said under my breath, thinking back to the many times Santa forgot to leave gifts at our house.

After we paid for our food, we started on our journey again. The new tires I had bought a few days before made the drive really smooth, and I imagined we were floating down the highway on the clouds. The leaves were beginning to turn colors, and blended together creating a radiant masterpiece. Every few minutes momma would blurt out, "This is a great time to take a trip. I'm getting a chance to see the fall foliage. Oh, Benita! Look at the colorful leaves on that tree!"

Although it was raining when we first left home, during most of our journey, the sun was screaming and boldly made its presence known. As we got closer to Kansas City, the clouds appeared again, and a few showers here and there, resulted in a beautiful rainbow in the sky. Each color seemed to perfectly blend into the next. And like a little girl, I named all the colors in my head, "Yellow, orange, red, green, and blue!"

When we reached Grandview, Missouri, I noticed the road construction had been completed. For the past five years, there had been road blocks, a two lane highway, and slower speed limits for at least twenty miles before we reached the main highway to Sharon's apartment. Momma had left the directions at home, so we took the wrong exit. We recalled taking the wrong exit once before, and then, turned around and got back on the right highway.

Once we reached Sharon's apartment, her adorable granddaughter, Alivia, met us on the porch and shyly greeted us with a smile. We eagerly followed her inside as though she was our personal tour guide.

We were delighted to watch Alivia walk freely about her grandmother's home as she talked in a language that only she understood. After awhile, she handed me several small books that contained short phrases of wisdom. Even though I wanted to relax after our long drive, I managed to read through them quickly. But when Alivia saw I had finished reading, as though it was "Divine Intervention," she gently handed me a book about courage, and then, walked away as if her assignment was complete.

After Alivia's mother picked her up, Sharon took us to eat at our favorite barbecue place. I slowly dipped my French-fries in the barbecue sauce before taking a bite. As I washed it down with strawberry pop, I closed my eyes to take a mental picture of the flavor.

Momma had some dental work completed a few days before we left for Kansas City, so I wasn't sure if she would be able to enjoy the taste of the succulent ribs.

"You can dip your French-fries in the sauce and just suck off the sauce!" I suggested, as I laughed uncontrollably.

"At least that way you'll still be able to taste the delicious flavor!"

But of course, momma wasn't going to let a few fillings stop her from eating her favorite barbeque. She had waited too many years for this opportunity!

Once we finished eating, we took off to see the city lights. We drove slowly down *Eighteenth Street*; my parents' old stumping grounds. I envisioned the streets filled with people dancing and dressed in only white from head to toe, from the *White Linen* party I had seen on a previous trip. The area had been redeveloped, and I could feel the excitement as the sound of Jazz and Blues music filled the air. Just as a doctor puts the stethoscope against his patient's chest to listen to the heart beat, I rolled down my window to hear the beat of the city.

We went downtown to see the *Blue Light District*. Trees were lit up with blue Christmas lights that brightly lit up the city streets. Though the night air was cold, no one seemed to notice. Lovers were holding hands, and friends were talking to each other with excitement as they headed toward the Sprint Center. Janet Jackson was in concert that night, and people were anxiously rushing to make sure they didn't miss a minute of what was sure to be an effervescent performance.

Our next stop was *The Plaza*. It was also filled with sparkling lights, dancing water fountains, and people riding in horse driven carriages. It seemed like we were retracing my footsteps from childhood. However, this time, the footsteps were leading me to a different perspective and a new sense of freedom; as though one season was ending and a new one beginning.

Once we arrived back at Sharon's apartment, I found a cozy spot to relax and read the book Alivia had given me. As I read, I quickly became captivated, but after reading only a few pages I fell asleep.

We woke up early the next morning because momma wanted to go to garage sales. As we went from sale to sale, I read the book in between helping to find the address to each sale. I had a hard time trying to keep momma and Sharon quiet; they talked like there was no tomorrow. "I'm going to put both of y'all in a time out, if y'all don't quiet down!" I jokingly interrupted. All the while, I had been trying to keep them quiet, so I could read as much as I could before we went back home.

Around two o'clock I began to get hungry, so I grabbed a few pieces of chocolate at one of the houses having a sale. Since they were free, I really wanted to take a handful, but only took a few so I wouldn't spoil my appetite. We finally pulled momma away from the garage sales an hour later, and headed to the mall. We ate lunch and relaxed for awhile, so we could continue to look for more good deals.

After we returned from shopping, I continued reading, but just like the night before, I found myself nodding off to sleep. I made a mental note to add the title to the list of books that were already a part of my goal to read twenty-five books before the end of the year. Before I fell asleep, I practiced in my mind how I was going to persuade Sharon to let me take the book home with me.

At six-thirty the next morning, my eyes popped wide open like the "Jack in the Box" toy after being wound up by an overly active child. I realized the book contained answers to some questions that were still lingering in the back of my mind. I now understood that because of my fears, I had lost sight of my "true" self—the "powerful, courageous, and confident" self that God created me to be.

"How ironic," I thought to myself. "I am *here* in Kansas City, the place where it all began as a little girl—the place where I began locking my pain deep within my soul. No wonder I woke up without an alarm clock this morning feeling rejuvenated. My soul is being emancipated from the clutches of bondage that kept me enslaved for so many years!"

In the past, I would lock up my emotions like a prisoner behind bars, while at other times my emotions would be all over the place, like a roller coaster wildly out of control. Each time I gained more knowledge about the traumatic life events I experienced, my soul was breaking free. This new sense of freedom caused me to laugh within myself because I realized, like pieces of a puzzle, the understanding of my "purpose" was miraculously coming together.

Usually, when I visited Kansas City, I always wanted to go back to the place I grew up, back to my old house and my old neighborhood, as though I was looking for something, or expecting something magical to happen. Maybe I was looking for answers to my many questions about who this *Benita Louise* really is.

After driving over the city the past few days, seeing the new sights, the new lights, and feeling the new vibe, I had no desire to go back to my old house on this trip. I wanted to hold on to the excitement and the pulsating beat of Kansas City that was flowing through my mind. I planned to use the positive energy to continually ignite the enthusiasm and passion I would need for the many years to come!

〜⚬〜⚬〜

From childhood to adolescence, teenager to adult, and married to single parent, I had been constantly under construction. God allowed the wrong turns, the tears, the pain, and the disappointments to drill and chisel deep down in my soul and uncover the things that had me weighted down.

When I ventured off the road, the "Word of God" was the map that guided me back to the right path. Every word of encouragement spoken to me, every helping hand that helped me, every prayer I prayed, and every prayer that was prayed for me, provided light during the darkest nights along my journey!

As momma and I began our journey back home, again, we made a wrong turn and ended up on the wrong highway. And again, we simply turned around and found the right way.

"I hope we didn't lose too much time by turning around," momma stated calmly.

"Nope, none at all," I said with a smile on my face. Because *now*, I knew without a doubt, my wrong turns were missing pieces of the puzzle that were all a part of my journey.

Chapter 22

⁓

EXTENDED WARRANTY
Letting Go

B EFORE I LEFT Kansas City, I convinced Sharon to let me borrow the book about courage that Alivia had innocently placed in my hands. I knew it contained valuable keys that would unlock the chains that had me bound for many years, and propel me into my destiny, enthusiastic and full of life.

Once I returned home, during each moment of free time I had my head buried in the book, as though I was looking for lost treasure. As I read, I could feel myself being strengthened and set free, as though weights were literally being lifted off my shoulders. Distorted thought patterns were being eradicated and new levels of understanding and wisdom about my purpose were being revealed.

⁓⁓⁓

When Raymond moved back home, we didn't discuss how long he planned to stay with me. (*This should have been the first topic of discussion*). We both agreed he would save money to buy a new car, and of course, establish the *must-have* emergency fund. He also agreed to pay rent each week, and to pay back the money he had borrowed over the past few years.

As time went by, Raymond was clearly enjoying having extra money in his pocket and buying new clothes. Even though he followed my house rules, each time he did something that agitated me; I would make a suggestion for him to start looking for his own place.

Because Raymond was still living under my roof, I was concerned that he wasn't experiencing life as a young man his age should. I knew there were "life lessons" he needed to learn in his twenties and that as he grew older, it would be hard for him to change any irresponsible mindsets. And the last thing I wanted was for him to get comfortable while staying with me, because I knew it could set him back even more.

Occasionally, a question like: "Raymond is your room clean?" would spring up out of nowhere, and I knew this definitely wasn't a question a mother should be asking her adult son. Although I realized Raymond being at home was not preparing him to be a responsible husband and father, the idea of him paying me back the money he owed, and also paying rent, overshadowed all my logic.

≤≤≤

From time to time, Raymond would make a casual comment that he was going to move out, and of course I would get excited. When the time came for him to move, he would give me an excuse and want to stay an additional two weeks. Although this disappointed me, I patiently waited for the time to pass.

As I continued to read the book about courage, I gained a different perspective of Raymond living at home. I realized we both wanted our own homes, but we had developed an emotional dependency toward each other that made it hard for us to sever our ties. I also felt that he had become too relaxed, and had activated an unwritten "extended warranty" policy that allowed him to still be at home at age twenty-six.

Whenever Raymond planned to be out late, he stayed out until the next day so he wouldn't disturb my sleep. One Saturday night while he was out with his friends, I curled up on the couch to relax and read a book. Although I fell asleep faster than usual, I woke up after sleeping for what seemed only a few hours. When I realized it was three o'clock in the morning I tried to go back to sleep, but after a few minutes I began to toss and turn. I decided if I wasn't asleep in an hour, I would get up and start doing some work around the house.

As I lay in bed, thoughts began to flash across my mind like an airplane leaving a written message in the sky: "Why do you keep letting Raymond do this? He is not going to leave home the way you want him to. He is comfortable and he needs you to put a demand on his potential. He is an adult and very capable of taking care of himself. The experiences he will gain and lessons he will learn being on his own, will far outweigh the money he is paying you. You don't want him to end up paying you all the money he owes you and still not be self-sufficient. If he doesn't move out now, he will get stuck in a pattern of depending on you, and even worse, you depending on him. You won't go broke without him paying you rent. You will be fine and he will be fine, too. You have equipped him to be a responsible adult. All you have to do is let go of your fears!"

At that moment, as swift as the eagle flies, I jumped out of bed and began packing my son's clothes. I knew I had to move fast before any sign of fear appeared, that would cause me to change my mind. I had packed my son's clothes before while in a moment of emotional anger, but this time I had total peace. I knew my son was at a good place in his life—he was happy and being responsible, so I knew *this* time it was right. I quickly put his clothes in the big tubs where he kept some of his things. Whatever I couldn't fit in the tubs, I neatly stacked in boxes in the living room.

By the time I finished packing, it was six o'clock in the morning. After neatly placing everything in one corner, I attempted to get some sleep. "My class at church starts in a few hours," I said to myself. "I just started this class and I can't miss. I don't know how I'm going to make it."

After I had been asleep for only an hour, my eyes popped open as though an alarm clock was going off in my head. I stumbled off the couch and began to put on my clothes.

"No studying the memory verse for me this morning, and definitely no time for a hot cup of tea to get me started," I muffled under my breath. So, to encourage myself to keep moving, I reached deep within my soul for strength, and stated: "Okay, Benita, you can do this! Just two hours of class and you can come home and get back in the bed!"

On my way to class, I decided to contact Raymond to let him know there had been a change in the plans for his date to move out. I had locked both of the doors and I didn't want him to come home and see his things packed. I'm sure seeing his clothes in boxes would have definitely sent him over the edge, and rightly so. After all, *this time*, he hadn't done anything wrong. Instead of calling him, I sent him a text message and briefed him on a few of the details:

> Son, u r a man and u need 2 b on your own. I have found a place 4 u 2 stay til your apartment is ready. Call me when u get this. We can find a place 2 meet so we can talk about this. The front door is locked.

♪♪♪♪

Class was over at ten-thirty. I was on my way home when Raymond called. He had gone to his grandmother's since he couldn't get in the house.

"Momma, I don't understand why you packed my things when I didn't do anything wrong," he calmly stated.

"Raymond, I will call you back after I get something to eat!" I said in a hurry, not wanting to deal with the issue. But instead of calling him back, I decided to go to the eleven o'clock service to prolong our discussion.

After church was over, I called Raymond and told him to meet me at the restaurant up the street from our house. I always preferred a neutral environment when it came to discussing serious issues; besides, discussing the situation at home would give him the upper hand. With Raymond being an excellent debater, he would know exactly how to get me to change my mind. He always knew just what to say and how to say it, to convince me to do something he wouldn't dare ask a man. After I realized what he had done, I would become upset with myself for being a pushover and unwise to his clever tactics.

A few minutes later, we arrived at the restaurant. He got in my car and proceeded to ask why I packed up his things. "This is not the way to handle issues, mother," Raymond stated with no emotion.

"Son . . .," I began to say with not much voice tone, "you haven't done anything wrong. There is no problem. You are a man and it's time for you to get your own place. You *are* being responsible and I am so proud of you." I was so tired from only getting three hours of sleep, that the words were coming out of my mouth at a snails pace.

"But mom . . .!" Raymond exclaimed as he began to state his case.

I quickly interrupted him and gave one of the best *Academy Award* winning performances ever.

"Son, can't you see momma is so tired . . .? I don't have anything left. I have found a place for you to stay, or you can stay with my brother until your apartment is ready."

"Okay mom. Can I have the money back that I paid you for rent? I'm paid up until next Wednesday."

Raymond followed me back to the house to get some of his things. He didn't tell me where he planned to stay, and I never asked.

A week later when Raymond's apartment was ready, Jeremiah, his cousin, helped him move. I watched them load up my couch and queen size bed onto the truck, while trying to make sure I didn't seem too excited that he was finally moving.

"I'll call you when I get to my apartment!" he stated anxiously, as they pulled off.

I stood at the door and watched them drive away. When they turned the corner, the biggest smile I ever smiled magically appeared on my face. I slowly walked back into the house and glanced at the empty rooms. It didn't matter to me that my house was empty and it looked as though I was the one starting over. And, I began to dance and shout, and laugh hysterically.

In reality, Raymond and I were both starting over. He was beginning his own journey, and I was moving to the next stage of my life with a new perspective. I finally had the courage to let go of my fears, and boldly pursue my goals and dreams. I not only survived single parenting, I *victoriously* lived to tell about it!

Author's Afterthoughts

ONCE I REPLACED my unrealistic expectations and distorted beliefs with what I called "power thoughts," I had the ability to change my life. I quickly realized if my perception of "this place" in life was a physical place with material success, or if I always expected life's conditions to be perfect, I would always be on a grueling, never-ending search for a place that didn't exist.

Now, I understand life to be a journey; a series of experiences that teach life lessons. "This place" in life has become a "rest" in God—a complete trust in His Sovereignty. As I continue my pursuit of finding God, I am confident in knowing I will find my purpose, as the gifts He has placed in me, inexorably unfold.

Along my journey, there were issues that engulfed my world; issues that tossed me here and there like a rag doll being carried around by a two year old. These issues moved me from place to place like a leaf when the wind blows, traveling uncontrollably without direction.

In God's Sovereignty, these issues created a passion in me like a fire that can't be quenched. This very passion, God knew would drive me to write this book, and to help others break free from the bondage that keeps them from accomplishing their goals and dreams, and pursuing the purpose for which they were created!

~~~

Notes

Chapter 20 — Introducing Amy

1. Gregory Berns, "Iconoclast: *A Neuroscientist Reveals How to Think Differently* (Harvard Business Press, 2008).

2. Ibid.

3. Ibid.

4. Ibid.

5. Ibid.

6. Ibid.

7. Ibid.

Suggested Reading

Dr. Caroline Leaf, "Who Switched Off My Brain: *Controlling Toxic Thoughts and Emotions,* (Switch On Your Brain USA Inc., 2008). Website: www.drleaf.net

Gregory Barns, "Iconoclast: *A Neuroscientist Reveals How to Think Differently,* (Harvard Business Press, 2008).

To book speaking engagements, visit us online at:

www.benitalouise.com

LaVergne, TN USA
22 April 2010
180145LV00001B/5/P